P9-AOY-431

# Everyday Symbols
# for Joyful Living

Dianne Durante, Ed.S.

Illustrations by Kelly Cabrera

*Everyday Symbols for Joyful Living* © 2008
by **Dianne Durante, Ed.S.**

Published By:

PO Box 112050
Naples, Florida 34108-1929

Toll Free: 1-877-513-0099 (in U.S. and Canada)
Phone: (239) 513-9907
Fax: (239) 513-0088

**www.QoLpublishing.com**

Cover photography by Nora Scarlett Studio, Inc.

**ISBN 10: 0-9675532-7-X**
**ISBN 13: 978-0-9675532-7-6**

**Library of Congress Control Number: 2005909297**

First Printing

All rights reserved. No part of this book may be reproduced without prior permission of the publisher.
Printed in the United States of America.

## To My Two Role Models:

My mother, Ami Durante,
Who gave me the greatest gift
—LIFE—
And then showed me how to live
With love, dedication, and hard work;

And my daughter, Kirsten Hagman,
Who gave me the greatest reason for living
—LOVE—
And challenges me to live a life of freedom and passion.
You're the best!

And to the memory of my Dad, Leo,
The wind beneath my wings, who guides me from heaven
With his laughter and saxophone.

# Contents

Acknowledgments     ix

Introduction:     The Beginning     1

Symbol One:     A Penny     5

Chapter 1     **A Penny — Communication**     6
Activities for Enhancing Communication     9

Chapter 2     **A Penny — Two Sides**     11
Activities for Seeing Different Sides     13

Chapter 3     **A Penny — More than Luck**     16
Activities for Developing an "I Can" Attitude     20

Chapter 4     **A Penny — Money Dynamics**     22
Activities for Understanding Your Money Dynamics     26

Chapter 5     **A Penny — In God We Trust**     28
Activities for Developing Spiritual Insight     31

Symbol Two:     A Chocolate Heart     35

Chapter 6     **A Chocolate Heart — Chocolate = Love + Health**     36
Activities for Experiencing the Pleasures of Chocolate     39

Chapter 7     **A Chocolate Heart — Caring Contact and Connection**    40

Activities for Creating Caring Contact and Connection    45

Chapter 8     **A Chocolate Heart — Passion**    46

Activities for Arousing Passion    50

Chapter 9     **A Chocolate Heart — It Is What's Inside that Counts**    52

Activities for Unwrapping the Foil    55

## Symbol Three:    An Elastic Band     **59**

Chapter 10     **An Elastic Band — Risk**    60

Activities for Developing Appropriate Risk-Taking    64

Chapter 11     **An Elastic Band — Resiliency**    66

Activities for Developing Resiliency    70

Chapter 12     **An Elastic Band — Stretch**    72

Activities for Stretching the Body    75

## Symbol Four:    A Pencil     **79**

Chapter 13     **A Pencil — Written Communication**    80

Activities for Enlivening Written Communication    84

Chapter 14     **A Pencil — Emotional Release**    86

Activities for Releasing Emotions    89

Chapter 15     **A Pencil — Erase It**    91

Activities for Erasing Mistakes and Moving On    94

## Symbol Five: A Crayon    **99**

| | | |
|---|---|---|
| Chapter 16 | **A Crayon — Play** | 100 |
| | Activities for Developing Playfulness | 103 |
| Chapter 17 | **A Crayon — Color Your World** | 105 |
| | Activities for Coloring Your World | 108 |
| Chapter 18 | **A Crayon — Creativity** | 110 |
| | Activities for Developing Creativity | 114 |

## Symbol Six: A Candle    **119**

| | | |
|---|---|---|
| Chapter 19 | **A Candle — Keep It Light** | 120 |
| | Activities for Keeping It Light | 124 |
| Chapter 20 | **A Candle — Ritual** | 126 |
| | Activities for Enhancing Your Life Through Rituals | 131 |
| Chapter 21 | **A Candle — Aging Gracefully** | 133 |
| | Activities for Aging Gracefully | 137 |

## Symbol Seven: A Seashell    **141**

| | | |
|---|---|---|
| Chapter 22 | **A Seashell — Protection** | 142 |
| | Activities for Creating Protection | 145 |
| Chapter 23 | **A Seashell — One of a Kind** | 146 |
| | Activities for Celebrating Your Unique Qualities | 149 |

| | | |
|---|---|---|
| Chapter 24 | **A Seashell — Mother Nature** | 151 |
| | Activities for Connecting to Mother Nature | 155 |

# Closing: Your Everyday Symbols     **159**

**Epilogue**     160

**BiblioTherapy**     161

**Websites**     166

**Index**     167

**About the Author**     179

**About the Illustrator**     181

# Acknowledgments

This little book had BIG helpers, and to them I owe a gigantic THANK YOU!

There are some people who make the world better just by being in it. Publisher Karla Wheeler is one of those people. Since 1998, she has been a friend, consultant, project manager, and enthusiastic cheerleader for me and my books. Her hard work, guidance, and belief in my dreams made this book a reality. I believe she was sent to me by angels. I know her gifts make this world a better place.

She has introduced me and my book to her talented troupe of angels. Special thanks to Dashia Larimer, who led the project through many revisions and kept smiling. Thanks also to Carole Greene, Traceé Young, Jill H. Lawrence, Amanda Grace, Kurt Wisner, Kathy Wisner, and Sandra Yeyati, who blessed the book with their editing skills. Thank you to Kelly Cabrera, angel artist extraordinaire, who has blessed these pages with her magic touch. Special thanks to Lane Hawley Cole for her encouragement and editing of the initial "Happiness" manuscript. Finally, thanks to Mark May, who designed the bright, beautiful cover.

*—Dianne Durante*

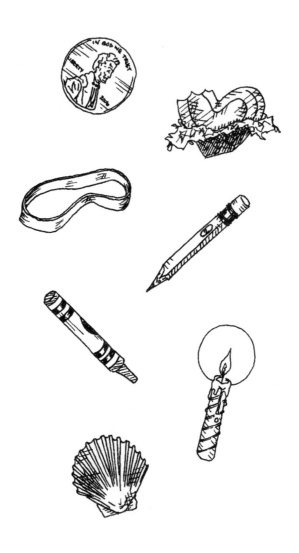

# The Beginning

It was 1991. I was invited to lecture to 350 seventh grade students. My task was to motivate and inspire them. My daughter was one of the students in the audience, and she was less than enthusiastic about my appearance as the keynote speaker. She chided me, "If you embarrass me, I'll die on the spot."

With that added pressure, I knew I needed to find some special way to connect with these teens. My magic wand was on loan to my fairy godmother, my broomstick was broken, and my ideas were drying up.

Then I remembered the saying, "A picture is worth a thousand words." Brain research reveals that we are more likely to remember what we see than what we hear. Just imagine the magic if we involve **more** senses. So began my journey with symbols.

As a marriage and family therapist, I was trained in the use of metaphors and symbols. I use them daily in my work because they are suggestive and powerful tools for transformation. The word "symbol" comes from the Greek word "sym," meaning *with* or *together* and "bollein," meaning *to throw* or *draw*. Symbols have a unique way of drawing things together. They create connections. We attach meanings to them that may vary from culture to culture, yet regardless of our customs, symbols have one thing in common: they stand for something else. The power of symbols lies in their ability to stir up memories and emotions. They touch our hearts and our minds.

My approach using everyday symbols, such as a penny, pencil, elastic band, and candle, worked that fateful day many years ago when my daughter sat in the auditorium filled with middle school students. The teenagers immediately responded to my interactive session, which asked them to consider what a penny might mean in their lives. How about a stretchy elastic band? Or even a little candle one uses on a birthday cake?

This was the beginning of my "Happiness: It's in the Bag!™" lectures. For over sixteen years I have lectured to folks of all ages about symbols and their universal meanings, often giving audience members brown bags filled with any number of small objects, from pennies to seashells.

I hope these symbols inspire you to get back to the basics of happy living so you can enjoy a more fulfilling life and not feel overwhelmed by the complexities of society.

Together we will explore the insights offered by a fun and creative interaction with seven everyday items:

- A Penny
- A Chocolate Heart
- An Elastic Band
- A Pencil
- A Crayon
- A Candle
- A Seashell

These simple items are used in this book to symbolize fundamental principles for joyful, balanced living.

Activities at the end of each chapter provide practical ways you can incorporate the basic concept of each symbol into your daily life.

Insights into communication, perspective, positive thinking, faith, creativity, humor—these are just a few of the many morsels of wisdom that await you.

Enjoy!

### SYMBOL ONE

# A Penny

# A Penny

## Communication

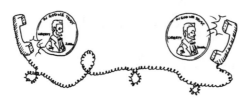

When you think about the first symbol, the penny, perhaps the old saying, "A penny for your thoughts," comes to mind. This phrase emphasizes the importance of *communication*, sharing our thoughts and ideas with others. When we share, a listener needs to be present, as well as a speaker. How often in our daily lives do we hear people rattling off their thoughts, always talking, but with no one listening?

> To **hear**(t) with the **heart** and the (h)**ear**(t) is an (he)**art**.
>
> – *Cliff Durfee*

Imagine the secrets that stay locked within us because we cannot find someone to open their ears and hearts to hear us. I tell people I have the best job in the world; I am paid to listen! My day is spent listening to the secrets that people have locked within. I am honored to be able to listen with an understanding ear. I know most of you also have this capacity but don't always take the time to listen carefully to what is being said.

Try these three simple listening basics:

- Make eye contact. Look at the person who is speaking.
- Lean forward.
- Keep your mouth closed—ears and eyes open. Remember, the same letters are in both words—you must get S-I-L-E-N-T to L-I-S-T-E-N.

We don't have to provide a solution to their problem or offer a wise comment. Usually, people just want to be heard, so practice listening.

> The first duty of love is to listen.
>
> — *Paul Tillich*

Do we remember to listen to ourselves? A penny for your thoughts and my thoughts, too. How important it is to pay attention to ourselves. When we value what we say to ourselves, others will value what we say to them. So much of our self talk is negative and critical. We compare ourselves to others and usually come up "less than" or "not as good." Wouldn't it be wonderful if we could stop the comparisons and be in our own corner, cheerleading for ourselves? We can!

When you talk to yourself, talk in positive terms. Encourage yourself. Compliment yourself. Pat yourself on the back for a job well done. Pay extra attention to what you say to yourself in times of distress or adversity.

One final word on communication. Often in therapy, when couples come in, one partner will say, "I shouldn't have to tell her what I want, we've been together for nine years. She should know." Get serious! No one is a mind reader. We need to take responsibility for ourselves and ask for what we need. Communicate it clearly. We also need to ask other people what they need from us. So often in relationships, listening and being present are tough. Asking takes courage and trust. So be brave—and ask!

"A penny for your thoughts" reminds us to communicate clearly.

# Activities for Enhancing Communication

1. **Learn to listen.** 𝔇

   You have two ears and one mouth. Use them in that ratio.

   a) Pick a day and practice listening. Imagine you have laryngitis and can't talk. Listen for one day without talking.

   b) Actively listen, repeat what people say, and then state your comment.

   *Example:*

   *Tom complains, "What a terrible day at work!"*

   *Mary responds, "Sounds like you really had an awful day. Do you want to talk about it?" Then she listens. Later, Mary asks Tom for a few minutes to share her thoughts.*

2. **Understand body language.** 🕴

   Your body language can "speak" with more impact than your words. Imagine you are on TV, and watch yourself as you talk to others. Notice your facial expressions, where your arms are, your eye contact. "I love you" said with your arms crossed is a lot different than "I love you" said in an embrace, looking deeply into your loved one's eyes.

   Experts indicate that communication is:

   56%   body language
   36%   tone of voice
    8%   *actual words!*

3. **Explore different types of communication.**

Pay attention to the three levels of communication:
- What you mean to say
- How you say it—tone and body language
- How the listener interprets what you have said

4. **Learn and use 'I messages.'**

An "I message" is a simple, clear, and effective form of communication, especially when you have strong feelings about an issue. The following format is good for an "I message."

"When you (*describe action*), I feel (*state your feeling*), because (*how action affects you*). What I need from you is (*describe behavior you want from person*)."

This helps the communicator clearly describe the offensive behavior and *accept her feelings* as a result of the behavior.

*Example:*

*Mary explains to Tom, "When you are late for dinner, I feel scared, because I am afraid you may have gotten into an accident. What I need is for you to call if you will be more than thirty minutes late."*

# CHAPTER 2

# A Penny

## Two Sides

I used to teach a college sociology course called "Love and Relationships." In class, I held up a penny and invited suggestions from the students on how this penny could symbolize something we need in life. One of them, a police officer, suggested, "A penny has two sides, and you need to remember to look at both sides." How true.

> Minds are like parachutes: they only function when they're open.
>
> — *Thomas Dewar*

Actually, we must remember to look at *numerous* sides of an issue. Brainstorm. Be creative. Explore many dimensions to find a resolution to your problems. Expand your vision. Call in experts, if need be. Talk to friends. Consciously look for viewpoints different from yours.

Consider what your adversaries would do. In fact, talk to people who disagree with you and listen to find out how they arrived at their conclusions. Take in as much information as you can. Broaden your vision.

When I work with couples in marriage counseling, they often get stuck and look at only their viewpoint. I make them change seats, actually sit in the other's chair, and repeat what they heard. Shifting viewpoints is not that easy, but it can make a big difference. If it's hard to understand another's point of view, visualize yourself holding the thought in your hands, away from your body. Don't take it personally. Imagine you are a mediator trying to hear both sides.

> The best way to have a good idea is to have lots of ideas.
>
> — *Linus Pauling*

It's healthy to try to look from another's perspective. It reminds us that people see the world as *they* are, wearing gray-, amber-, or rose-colored glasses. We set ourselves free of judgmental behavior when we choose a vision that respects differences. Everyone wins when we accept one another's right to freedom of choice.

Seeing from another's perspective could also activate your unconscious, and allow you to listen to your inner voice—your intuition. There are some

> Great Spirit, grant that I may not criticize my neighbor until I have walked a mile in his moccasins.
>
> — *Native American Saying*

conscious steps we can take to strengthen our intuition. Listen to your body. Your mind continually sends signals to your body. Try to become more attuned to the twinges—fleeting feelings of intuition. Keep an open mind. Pay attention to details and record what you notice. Developing your intuition takes time and effort, but it provides another amazing viewpoint for your decisions.

# Activities for Seeing Different Sides

1. **Agree to disagree.** ✹ ✹

   The next time you are in a heated conflict with someone, call a "time out" and say, "I guess we need to agree to disagree." This creates a win-win situation rather than a win-lose event. If a decision needs to be made, flip a coin (a penny) and whoever wins gets their way. Or you could solve conflicts by choosing even/odd days: Monday, Wednesday, Friday—it's your way; Tuesday, Thursday, Saturday—it's mine. This works great for minor family feuds.

2. **Walk a mile in their moccasins or wingtips.** 🐾

   a)  If you're alone:

   To view life from another perspective, imagine you *are* the other person. Stand or sit the way they do. Try to debate the issue from their viewpoint. Attempt to see and understand the issue from their perspective, with their background of experiences.

   b)  If you're with a friend:

   You need thirty minutes for this activity. Follow your friend (literally) as they go about their daily activities. Whether they are shopping or strolling through the park, walk behind and mirror them. Notice their breathing, their body motion or openness, and try to copy it. Then switch roles. Each person follows for ten minutes and then discusses what he or she has discovered.

3. **Brainstorm.** ✸

Sit with a group. Name the issue or problem you are exploring. List all of the ways this issue could be viewed, no matter how crazy or ridiculous. Let one idea lead you to another. Keep it flowing, and write down everything.

*Example:*

*My problem is that I'm broke, in debt, and need money. I could:*
- *Move to another state where there are more jobs*
- *Borrow from my family*
- *Borrow against my house*
- *Cut my expenses*
- *Have a roommate*
- *Enter a credit-counseling program*
- *Declare bankruptcy*
- *Sell my possessions and start over*
- *Work two jobs*
- *Go back to school*
- *Win the lottery*
- *Start a home business*

No censoring or comments at this point, just list everything that comes to mind. After you have explored all the options and made your list of all the sides, identify the ones you want to attempt, then try them.

## 4.  **Enhance your intuition.**  **?**

If you are interested in simple ways to be more aware and develop your intuition, I'd like to share two of mine. When I call my answering machine for messages, before I find out how many messages are waiting, I predict the number I will receive—two, three, four. When I hear the number, I can immediately validate my intuition. Or when my cell phone rings, before I pick it up, I guess who is calling. Try little ways to make daily predictions. Practice enhances our intuition.

# CHAPTER 3

# A Penny

## More Than Luck

"Find a penny, pick it up. All the day you'll have good luck." What is luck? According to *Webster's Ninth New Collegiate Dictionary*, luck is "the ability to prosper or succeed, especially through chance or good fortune." Yet, people who believe they are lucky act very differently than people who believe they are not lucky. It really is a mindset, a way of thinking, believing, and acting, that creates one's reality.

> If you think you can, or you think you can't, you're right.
>
> — *Henry Ford*

Our mind has tremendous power to affect our reality. Richard Wiseman, in his book *The Luck Factor,* identifies lucky people as those who are open and look for positive things. They also listen to lucky hunches/intuition and adjust their attitude to *expect* good fortune. They are able to be positive and resilient against misfortune.

In 1914, when Thomas Edison was sixty-seven years old, his New Jersey laboratory burned to the ground. Much of his life's work went up in spectacular flames that night. The next morning he looked at the ruins and declared, "There is great value in disaster. All our mistakes are burned up. Thank God we can start anew." Three weeks later, despite losing everything, he managed to finish one of his major inventions and was able to deliver his first phonograph.

What a difference an attitude of gratitude and positive thinking can make! Research shows us that optimists live longer and that positive emotions are needed for long-term memory. Being positive can lengthen our life and help us remember the wonderful life we have had.

> There are only two ways to live your life. One is as though nothing is a miracle, the other is as though everything is a miracle.
>
> — *Albert Einstein*

So, this "lucky" penny can represent the need to *think positively*. Our society has a difficult time with this concept. From our earliest years, we are taught to think, "What's wrong with me?" not, "What's right?" In school, teachers check off all the errors with red ink, rather than putting "C" for "correct" on all the answers that are right.

If we truly wanted to change and grow, we would focus much more on the positive. We would look for the healthy aspects of ourselves and others, rather than the unhealthy qualities. We would be mindful of the words we use and speak only in positive ways to others as well as to ourselves. We would use uplifting words to describe or label—words like "beautiful, smart," and "happy"—rather than destructive words such as "ugly, stupid," and "lazy." Uplifting words create a peaceful environment.

Remember that labels stick. Perhaps some of us have once said,

"Sticks and stones may break my bones, but words will never hurt me," and suffered in silence from unkind words. Words *do* hurt. They break our spirits, not our bones.

> If you judge people, you have no time to love them.
>
> — *Mother Teresa*

Years ago I heard a wonderful story about a little boy who was often angry and spoke mean words to others. One day, his father gave him a bag of nails and a hammer. Dad said, "Every time you want to say something mean or angry, go out to the backyard and hammer nails into the fence."

So the little boy did just that. Days and weeks passed, and the boy hammered. It was hard work. Soon he was able to control his anger and his tongue, and he returned to his father and said, "I'm much kinder and not as angry now, Dad. Can I stop hammering?"

His father answered, "Yes, you may stop. But now, every day you are kind and control your temper, please take out one nail."

Finally the boy had removed all the nails.

The father took his son by the hand and they went to look at the fence together. "You have done well, my son; but look at the holes in the fence. The fence will never be the same. When you say mean things, they leave a scar just like these holes in the fence. No matter how many times you say, 'I'm sorry,' the wound is still there."

Research on relationships has suggested that, for every negative comment, we need five positive comments to create a healthy balance. Often, when I have families in for therapy, each family member gets a chance to sit in the "honored person" spot and receive honor, respect, and praise for a few minutes. I can almost see this person growing an inch taller. The honored person must only listen and accept the positive comments, which is not an easy task. Family members rarely hear such praise and find it difficult, at first, to accept; however, everyone agrees that the positive feedback feels great.

Let the penny remind you to be optimistic and notice the positive in everyday life.

# Activities for Developing an 'I Can' Attitude

1. **Spend a day without denouncing anyone or speaking negatively.** 👄

   If we spoke to our friends as we do to our family, we'd have no friends. This Sunday, practice speaking kindly and positively to your family. Try to say only positive phrases:

   • "Walk carefully and slowly," instead of "Don't run."
   • "Remember your appointment," instead of "Don't forget."
   • "I need your help with the groceries," instead of "You're lazy; you never help."

2. **Think of your childhood and of all the names people called you (the labels).** 

   Which of those labels have stuck? Make a list and rename yourself in more positive terms.

   • Lazy—Relaxed
   • Slow—Methodical
   • Stubborn—Persistent
   • Hardheaded—Determined

3. **Change the labels.** ✒

   Think of your spouse, child, or a good friend. Turn all the negative labels imposed on them into positive ones.

4.  **Pay attention to your words.**

    For one day, list all the times you say, "No" or "I can't," and all the times you say, "Yes" or "I can." Strive to be an "I can" person.

# CHAPTER 4

# A Penny

## Money Dynamics

Apenny is just a penny, the smallest denomination of our currency. It is worth only one percent of a dollar. It is such a small unit of exchange that we rarely pay attention to it. Who stops to pick up a penny on the sidewalk anymore? Often, containers of pennies are kept by cash registers and "given" to customers to help make exact change.

> To generate prosperity in your own life, you must open your mind to it.
>
> — *Catherine Ponder*

The penny appears insignificant, but it is a reminder of an important relationship—with money. As a marriage counselor, I am often amazed that my clients disclose in dramatic detail their most intimate sexual secrets but rarely reveal their money secrets, concerns, or conflicts.

The relationship with money is such an emotionally volatile issue that it remains too private for many of us to share, even with a therapist (and certainly not with a significant other). This money relationship can be the most hostile and confusing relationship individuals have.

The money secrets, buried so deeply inside, begin to grow and control all aspects of our lives. Money secrets can be more destructive to a relationship than a sexual affair. Marriage counselors often identify money as "the other infidelity."

Our first teachers about money values are our parents. We often handle our money affairs the way we saw our parents handle theirs.

> Don't sacrifice your life to making a living.
>
> — *L. Giovannoni*

When I was growing up, I remember my parents fighting only once a month—when the checkbook needed to be balanced. My mother wanted to balance to the penny, while my father habitually forgot to tell her about checks he had written. When I married, I decided I didn't want to fight about money, so we never balanced the checkbook. Not a very wise financial decision, but we never fought over money.

For the past fifteen years, I have been offering money workshops for women. These programs are conducted with financial planners, family law attorneys, accountants, and me (a marriage counselor). I am amazed at the low level of knowledge and interest from married women on the topic of money. They still feel that managing money is a man's job. Women born before World War II seem to be most in the dark about money.

One of my mother's friends, Mary, found herself a widow at age eighty. She had never paid a bill or written a check. Mother wrote all of Mary's checks until Mary died five years later.

One of the saddest money cases I have ever encountered involved a sixty-five-year-old female client from my New Jersey practice. She arrived at my office one day in tears. Her seventy-year-old husband had just told her that they had no money left. They owned two large homes in very affluent communities, belonged to country and sailing clubs, and had been living very well. He controlled all the money, and she had no idea they were destitute. Her "ignorance is bliss" mentality turned into sudden death for her way of life.

People feel controlled by money, but we are actually controlled by fear. Fear blinds us and keeps us from looking openly at our relationship with money. Anything unknown can be fearful and mysterious. If we keep money locked in the deep, secret vault of fear, it will continue to cause pain and control us.

Money permeates every area of our lives. It represents power, freedom, and security. It defines who we are, where we live, what we do and don't do. It influences our dreams and goals.

We trade the time in our lives for money, so time *is* money. Yet we rarely stop long enough to realize what that means. If I spend eight hours working for one hundred dollars and then go out and buy a pair of designer shoes for ninety dollars, is that what I am working for? If we are going to trade time for money, let's make sure we value the things on which we spend the money, just as we value the time it took to earn it.

The penny reminds us to define and evaluate our relationship with money. Take control by learning about your finances. Invest in a money management course and take a look at how you might balance saving and spending. Be grateful for the prosperity that comes your way.

A penny reminds us to pay attention to our relationship with money. If you lead, you can have a delightful dance with money. Enjoy the dance.

# Activities for Understanding Your Money Dynamics

## 1. Watch your expenses. 👁

For one week, write down everything on which you spend money, down to the last penny. Carry a small notebook with you for accuracy. At the end of the week, take a sheet of paper and list your expenses in the appropriate categories.

| *Basic Needs* | *Wants/Desires* | *Pure Extravagance* |
|---|---|---|
| food at grocery store | movie tickets | chauffeured limousine |

What does the week's spending show you about what you value? How much life energy did you trade for wants and extravagances? Were they worth the price, both figuratively and literally?

## 2. Examine the money patterns you learned from your parents. 🍷

Write down the messages they gave you. Now rewrite some messages you'd like to give yourself.

*Example:*
*Old Message: "You'll never have enough money."*
*Rewrite: "I will have all the money I need in order to feel that my life is financially secure."*

Write the messages you are passing on to your children. If you don't have children, just pretend you do.

3. **Be aware of your actions.**

Notice how you react mentally and physically when you are in a bank or around wealthy people.

# CHAPTER 5

# A Penny

## In God We Trust

One last thought on the penny: "In God We Trust," written on the front side, is a reminder to trust in God or a higher power. What does it mean to trust in God? It means we have faith that there is a larger purpose or order in life.

Our forefathers founded this nation as a refuge for those who were persecuted for their beliefs. To them, the right to choose their religion was as vital as life itself. Over the past two hundred years, religion has continued to play a major role in America, though it has changed greatly. This is a country with diverse religious and spiritual practices.

Spirituality speaks to the soul, the core or center of each of us. Our values and

> The most beautiful thing we can experience is the mysterious. It is the source of all true art and science.
>
> — *Albert Einstein*

beliefs govern our existence and our actions. For many, these beliefs are private; others are more vocal. But almost all of us hold our spiritual notions dear to our hearts.

Some people express their spirituality through prayer, meditation, or the reading of scriptures. For others, art, literature, or music can speak to the soul. Many find spiritual awakening in their connection to nature or animals. Spirituality can be a combination of any and all of these. The renewal of our spirit through our spirituality refreshes our being and keeps us moving forward. It transforms our daily lives to a more meaningful existence of connection and oneness.

> We are not human beings having a spiritual experience. We are spiritual beings having a human experience.
>
> — *Teilhard de Chardin*

Spirituality and prayer possess proven benefits. A Duke University study in 2002 found that people with strong spiritual beliefs tend to live longer, are more energetic, and less likely to feel depressed or anxious. People who pray or meditate experience the relaxation response—a drop in blood pressure, heart rate, and levels of stress hormones. In the brain, alpha and theta waves increase, suggesting deeper relaxation levels. Every day more research studies conducted by major teaching universities are validating the effect of prayer and meditation on healing.

Many of us have our own experiences to share. Several years ago, when my mother was eighty-nine years old, she was diagnosed with advanced lung cancer and given three to six months to live. We explored many treatment options, but she made the decision to continue her life without any medical treatments. She had been blessed with a vibrant, healthy life to that point and hoped to make it to her ninetieth birthday. Mother continued her active daily schedule that started every day with morning mass. Her name was put on every prayer list, regardless of denomination—Baptist, Jewish, Unitarian, Buddhist—all prayed and meditated for her healing. Today, at ninety-five, she still sprinkles our life with her energy and love, as well as two to three Italian meals a week!

More and more, we are a society that values spiritual knowledge. Two years ago I was flying from Frankfurt, Germany, to Rome, Italy. I sat next to a nice young man, and we began talking. He said that he was a caretaker for Sir John Templeton's estate and that Sir John Templeton had set aside thirty million dollars a year to fund scientific projects exploring the nature of God.

One look at the bestseller list in recent years shows a society clamoring for insight into our inner lives, our souls, and even life after death.

Mother Teresa said, "We need to find God, and He cannot be found in noise and restlessness. God is the friend of silence. See how nature—trees, flowers, grass—grows in silence; see the stars, the moon, the sun, how they move in silence. We need silence to be able to touch our souls."

> The real voyage of discovery consists not in seeking new landscapes but in having new eyes.
>
> *— Marcel Proust*

The "In God We Trust" inscription on a penny reminds us to trust in a higher power.

# Activities for Developing Spiritual Insight

1. **Let a circle represent your life.** O

   There are four aspects of life to consider: physical, mental, emotional, and spiritual. Divide the circle to show how much time you spend daily in each area. Do you feel comfortable with the division? What would you change? This week, make an effort to spend more time on your spiritual life and notice how it feels.

2. **Take a spiritual inventory.**

   What do you believe regarding reincarnation, life after death, tithing, angels, God, many gods, the Ten Commandments, Jesus as Savior, Buddha, Krishna, Mohammed, karma, faith, prayer, meditation, or the rosary?

3. **Define your spirituality.**

   What role does religion or spirituality play in your life? How do you define your spiritual life? What is your core spiritual belief? How important is it to you? Write a spiritual mission statement. Include any thoughts that are important to you.

4. **Describe your spiritual day.**

   Notice how your religious and/or spiritual beliefs manifest themselves in your daily life: in how you treat people, for instance, or in your diet, charitable giving, etc. Do you feel any conflicts between your beliefs and your actions or your beliefs and your desires?

*Example:*

*I'd like to try the ham sandwich at my favorite deli, but eating ham goes against my religion.*

5. **Learn about the spiritual lives of others.**

The next time you're with friends, ask them about their spiritual beliefs. Share who you are spiritually with a friend or family member and describe how your beliefs affect your daily life.

6. **Peruse collections of spiritual books.**

Browse through the spirituality section of your local bookstore and library. Read a copy of *Spirituality & Health* magazine.

# A Penny Reminds Us:

- To share our thoughts and listen with our ears and heart

- To look at both sides

- To develop an "I can," positive view of life

- To define and evaluate our relationship with money

- To develop and expand our spiritual insight

Please write down what a penny symbolizes to you. Keep a notebook or use the *Everyday Symbols for Joyful Living* workbook.

*Example:*

*Little things, like the penny, mean a lot. I need to pay more attention to little things like a smile, a "hello," a "thank you"—the basic courtesies of life.*

*SYMBOL TWO*

# A Chocolate Heart

# CHAPTER 6

# A Chocolate Heart

## Chocolate = Love + Health

We have known about the power of chocolate for a long, long time. The natives of Central and South America deserve our thanks for introducing us to chocolate. They worshipped chocolate, and it seemed to have dominated every facet of Aztec life, from sexuality to economy, as far back as 1100 B.C. Cocoa beans even served as currency.

Liquid forms of chocolate played a part in lovemaking rituals. Montezuma is said to have consumed tons of chocolate before visiting his harem. Those poor women! Casanova purportedly used chocolate as a prelude to lovemaking. Madame de Barry, Louis XV's mistress, served heavy doses of liquid chocolate to her suitors.

Cortés brought the dark substance to Spain, and by the seventeenth century, chocolate thrilled Europeans with its sensuous, stimulating, addictive qualities. If you could afford it, you drank it, sipping several cups a day. Doctors prescribed chocolate to lift spirits and raise libidos. No need for Viagra, just drink chocolate!

Chocolate was a liquid, luscious substance until the nineteenth century, when the Dutch found a way to separate cocoa butter, leaving powdered cocoa; and, yes, the chocolate bar became a reality. The bar began in Holland (Cadbury Brothers), moved to Switzerland (Nestle), then to America (Milton Hershey).

Chocolate produces a chemical in our bodies that mirrors the feeling of being in love. It increases our serotonin level, which helps us feel better. Goodbye depression, hello calories! The darker the chocolate and the higher the cocoa content, the more antioxidants to fight infection and keep us healthy.

Then, of course, there is the "chocolate high"—the buzz that comes because chocolate consists of more than three hundred natural chemicals. Eating a chocolate candy bar can be a lot like drinking coffee or having a small amount of espresso.

Research shows that dark chocolate can produce better blood flow. Eating three ounces of dark chocolate a day might even lower blood pressure. It contains polyphenol flavonoids, which are heart-healthy substances.

Chocolate abounds with healing properties for both our body and our soul. But its addictive qualities can wreak havoc on our lives. The main problem with chocolate, of course, is that it is not a controlled substance, and we must monitor and control our own intake. Too much of a good thing—even chocolate—can be harmful, not healthy.

While writing this book and lecturing for the last dozen years, I will tell you I cannot keep chocolates in my house. Once I start, it is very difficult for me to stop eating them. The chocolate brings up memories of many wonderful times, pleasant thoughts of celebrations and joyful moments. Today I have a healthy, happy heart, but the clothes in my closet are one size larger. If there is one food item I could not imagine living without, however, it's chocolate.

The taste, the texture, and the aroma of chocolate transport us to other worlds. Ah, the pleasures of the senses!

# Activities for Experiencing the Pleasures of Chocolate

1.  **There is only one activity.** 👄

    Savor a candy bar or a cup of hot chocolate. Enhance the experience by trying the following:

    *Step One*—Smell the chocolate. Take a deep, enriching breath and let the chocolate permeate your nostrils. Breathe deeply and enjoy the scent.

    *Step Two*—Take a small bite or sip of the chocolate. Hold it in your mouth. Close your eyes and savor the flavor.

*Enjoy!*

# CHAPTER 7

# A Chocolate Heart

## Caring Contact and Connection

The sweetness in a little foil-wrapped chocolate reminds me of many things. The first is the richness of a heart connection—the symbol of physical love and intimacy. (Passion is just around the corner, in the next chapter.) Physical caring and contact are essential, primal ingredients of a healthy life.

From the beginning of life, when a baby enters the world, we see the importance of touch for survival. Babies who are not routinely touched or held don't thrive like those who are. Premature babies in incubators also need to be given ample doses of caring touch. This nonverbal communication is so basic to life, from birth to death, that we cannot function normally without it.

Unfortunately, our society gives conflicting messages about touching. It's okay to cuddle and caress infants, but we cut off physical intimacy when children get older, out of the fear that all forms of touching are deemed sexual in nature! The early dismissal of touch in our lives and the lives of our children creates a society that starves for this essential ingredient and looks for ways to feed the hungry skin.

I am often amazed when I see families who were raised without this basic connection. In my Italian-American family we passed out hugs and kisses along with the pasta. It was second nature for me to hug and kiss someone when they arrived at our house. Only when I grew up and went away to college did I learn that not everyone had been so fortunate.

In my counseling practice I must ask permission to hug some clients because they have been abused, and *any* contact is frightening. We all have physical boundaries, and for some people their three-foot personal boundaries can never be intruded upon. As a therapist I understand it, but it makes me very sad.

Our touch-deprived society is searching for ways to fill the void. Some findings of the Delta Society on the influence of pets on human well-being might interest you. The findings show that pet owners have better psychological well-being and lower blood pressure. Pets decrease feelings of loneliness and isolation. Also, children's self-esteem is enhanced by owning a pet. The pet-industry boom is no accident. We have learned to substitute the "safe" petting of an animal for caressing our children and spouses. In many homes, even houseplants get more touch and communication than do members of the family.

> A friend is,
> as it were,
> a second self.
>
> — *Marcus Tullius Cicero,*
> De Amicitia

Another way we fill the "touch void" is with contact sports. Football, hockey, soccer, basketball, and even tag, have become the main modes of play at home. For too many children in our society, especially boys, horseplay, arm wrestling, and slaps on the back and rear end replace hugs and kisses. Sports are great, but they shouldn't be the only way our kids get positive physical feedback.

We live in a society filled with violence and distorted images of touching. For some, inappropriate touching has become better than no touching at all. I see children from abusive homes "acting out" or passing on the violence just to feel some skin contact or connection.

Jean and Harry Harlow's famous monkey studies showed that, without physical contact, monkeys become angry, frightened, and crazy. We humans act no differently. When we are deprived of touch, we feel angry, frightened, lost, depressed, despondent, and even abandoned. When we are touched lovingly, our muscles relax, tension is released, inner knots of frustration and isolation untie, and we feel connected again. This is a society in which sexual behavior, on average, begins at fourteen. Healthy physical contact from parents can help satisfy that basic human need and allow teenagers to wait until a more appropriate age before seeking physical intimacy.

"Have you hugged your kid today?" bumper stickers are a helpful reminder of the importance of physical intimacy in the lives of us all—the huggers as well as the huggees. Virginia Satir, a noted family therapist, once said we need four hugs a day for survival, eight hugs a day for maintenance, and twelve hugs a day for growth. I guess we all need to get busy!

The results of research on patients in hospitals and nursing homes illustrate the vital need for touch in the healing process. In the early phase of the AIDS epidemic, patients died from isolation and a lack of physical contact, as well as from the effects of the disease. Mother

Teresa and Princess Diana were two recent role models who demonstrated the value that touching sick people could have in healing both bodies and souls.

In 1989, my cousin Michael was dying of AIDS. He came from Los Angeles to New Jersey to visit me for the last time. He wanted to go to Broadway and see *The Phantom of the Opera*. He was pale and appeared tired and worn out—much older than his forty-five years. One day, as he rested, I sat down next to him and massaged his neck, shoulders, and head. His breathing slowed, he relaxed his body, and then tears ran down his cheeks. He said, "Thank you for your gentle touch. It means so much to me to feel connected now." Such a simple act can make such a difference.

> Leo Buscaglia (Dr. Hug) was one of the first ten inductees into the Hershey's Hugs Hall of Fame.

A 1997 American Medical Association (AMA) Research Study showed that these "human moments" can lower one's sensitivity to pain, as well as benefit the immune and cardiovascular systems. A feeling of "connectedness" was found to be a significant protective factor against violent behavior, severe emotional distress, suicide, and substance abuse. The good news, then, is that these human moments don't have to be lengthy to be beneficial. Actually, it's beneficial to both the giver and the receiver. So make connecting with others a priority.

The chocolate heart reminds us of another important connection. Just as physical touching is essential for healthy living, emotional touching is also vital. Emotional touching means to share yourself, listen with your heart, reach out and help your neighbor, and develop empathy for others.

Emotional connection provides families and friends with a special bond. In a society that is so transient, with families separated from one another by hundreds and even thousands of miles, the need for emotional connection with friends is imperative. Just remember that this kind of connection takes time; it doesn't happen overnight. Be patient and take the time. It's worth it.

Volunteering is another way to develop an emotional connection. It is good for the body and the soul. It helps us fill the "loneliness gap," while providing a wonderful service to others. Now that we retire at a younger age, with time and energy to spare, volunteering helps many people discover their purpose. Visits from volunteers can help the elderly keep going by giving them something to anticipate. Or, perhaps, you might want to become a mentor to a young person, or conduct nature walks at a botanical garden or park. Museums need volunteers as do libraries and schools. Assist in a clinic or blood bank. Maybe you love to sew. Why not make clothing for newborns or families in need? Volunteer opportunities are as endless as your imagination. Volunteering is a way of hugging the world.

The chocolate heart reminds us to find ways to hug the world with a heartfelt connection to ourselves and each other.

# Activities for Creating Caring Contact and Connection

### 1. Find out what's missing. ✎

List ways you can touch others, physically and emotionally. Who is important in your life? Call an old friend and reconnect. Let people know they are dear to you. Tell them—and show them.

### 2. Volunteer. ✋

Find an organization in which you believe and get involved. Even an hour a month makes a difference.

### 3. Identify your intimate activities. 🔍

Identify all the activities listed below that you currently do. Note some that you are willing to try to increase your intimacy level with others and yourself.

- Give a full-body massage
- Get a manicure
- Get a pedicure
- Exercise
- Swim
- Learn reflexology
- Hug someone

- Give a hand massage
- Give a neck massage
- Give a foot massage
- Cuddle with a child
- Pet an animal
- Treat a friend to a facial
- Cuddle with your partner

- Call a friend
- Write a letter to someone
- Hold hands
- Make love
- Go to lunch with a friend
- Laugh with someone
- Kiss

# CHAPTER 8

# A Chocolate Heart

## Passion

For centuries, the heart has been a symbol of romantic love. Valentine's Day plays on this symbol—chocolate hearts sell in all sizes. How interesting that we have selected one day out of 365 to focus on romantic love and passion. Imagine if we could make Valentine's Day every day and mix some Hershey's Kisses™ with those big, chocolate hearts. We could certainly stir up a lot of passion.

Passion, the central theme of this chapter, is one of the most important ingredients for a happy, healthy life. I define it as exuberance, euphoria, intense happiness that makes you feel on the edge, expectant, impulsive, yet strangely content. True passion is a joining of emotional energy and mental focus, a focus often so intense that nothing else seems to exist. It is a bubbling-over, infectious energy that makes each moment exciting.

> The aim of life is to live, and to live means to be aware, joyously, drunkenly, serenely, divinely aware.
>
> — *Henry Miller*

Passion implies commitment, dedication, and endurance.

We had the feeling as children. We were often absorbed for hours in play and fantasy. We were carried away in our world. Passion is a lot like many things: If we don't use it, we lose it. Like exercise, daily passion workouts can be energizing.

> Nothing great in the world has been accomplished without passion.
>
> — *G.W.F. Hegel*

I'll never forget seeing *The Today Show* when former President Jimmy Carter talked about some of his passions: painting landscapes and portraits, building furniture, writing a book a year, and making his own wine using a family recipe passed down from previous generations. And, he still found time to work for world peace and Habitat for Humanity. He certainly has been a great role model for exercising passion daily.

My father also relished his passion. He was a musician who loved to play the saxophone. In 1965, at the age of forty-five, he was diagnosed with Parkinson's Disease. Although the deterioration was slow, by age sixty-five he was doing poorly; he had to use a wheelchair and could hardly talk. Every week, however, my mother took him to play in the Ft. Lauderdale Big Band. She wheeled him straight to his seat, and he played his beloved saxophone. Even though his body betrayed him, his passion lived on and kept him going. Music helped keep his body more flexible and energized.

As adults, we seem to have no time for passions. We believe passion is for children or retirees, but not for working people consumed with the serious business of making a living.

Of course, it is more difficult at the peak of our work life to make passion a priority. If we don't, though, the quality of all our relation-ships (work, family, friends) will suffer from "passion deprivation." Passion can stir in any area of our lives. Perhaps you love your work and have a great deal of enthusiasm for it. Or maybe it's the week-ends for which you have a passion; you love boating, skiing, rock climbing, or gardening. It is essential to establish healthy passion pri-orities. Whatever your passions, relish them and make time for them. Thus begins the balancing act of transforming your passion *priority* list into a passion *reality* list.

As a marriage counselor, I'd like to take a moment to talk about sexual passion and intimacy. Relationships can also suffer from passion deprivation. In fact, finding time for sexual intimacy and passion is problematic in many marriages. A busy life, different schedules between husband and wife, children and other family responsibilities can make sexual intimacy a low priority. Couples feel they have no time for sex. Often we need to adjust our expectations of what a healthy sexual relationship is. Many things change, especially when we have children.

> Hold fast to dreams,
> for when dreams die,
> life is a broken-winged
> bird that cannot fly.
>
> — *Langston Hughes*

Sexual intimacy can be one of those things. Sometimes we have to make it fast—the quickies—while the kids are watching *Barney* or *Sesame Street*.

Quickies, like fast food, are not great for a steady diet but are okay if you are in a time crunch. Couples, however, need to plan for "fine dining" sex. Make an appointment, a date. Arrange babysitters; enlist family or friends. Try to arrange an entire evening to relax, reintroduce yourselves, and enjoy each other's company. After all the planning, you may not feel like it, but once you get started and allow yourself to relax, you will quickly recapture those "lost loving feelings."

It really is a matter of rethinking our priorities. Passion and sexual intimacy must be on the priority list. Too often it doesn't make the top ten list of things to do this week, or this month. Build intimacy by finding fun things to do together and talk about. Linda Ford and Beth Goodman wrote a wonderful little book called *The Owner's Manual.* This book is a good starting point for exploring each other. No matter how long you've been together, you can discover something new.

> When you put yourself wholeheartedly into something, energy grows. It seems inexhaustible.
>
> *— Helen De Rosis*

People change and they forget to tell each other. Take some time to reconnect with each other and rediscover passion. Make the bedroom alive and romantic again. Light scented candles. Display flowers. Unclutter the room (or hide the clutter). Listen to romantic music. Use massage oils and give each other foot massages or back rubs. And, of course, remember the chocolate.

The chocolate heart reminds us that passion, all kinds of passion, is a basic ingredient for a healthy life. It makes life so much more delicious.

# Activities for Arousing Passion

1. **List your passions.** 📄

   Make a list of twenty things you love to do (your passions). Note the last time you did each of them. If you aren't doing them, or haven't in a long time, start today. Create new passions: join the choir; take golf or tai chi lessons.

2. **Make a date.** 🗒

   Plan a special date with your partner or a friend. Do something you or they love to do.

3. **Move your body.** 🎵

   Put on your favorite music and dance! Movement is sensual and creates energized feelings. Music usually makes you feel better. Learn to play a musical instrument or relearn one you played as a child. Go to a concert.

4. **Learn new movements.** 🏃

   Take a ballroom or square dance class. Take tap or ballet lessons. Rent the movie *Shall We Dance?* with Richard Gere and dance to it!

5. **Explore new places.** 🏙

   Search for a new city or town or a new shop. Let yourself get "lost." Wander. Discover and enjoy with a friend. Share the passion of finding something new.

6. **Plan it out.** 📄

Plan a perfect romantic night. Decide on everything, from what you will wear to where you will go. Be specific, lavish, decadent. Plan and then JUST DO IT!

# CHAPTER 9

# A Chocolate Heart

## It Is What's Inside that Counts

Imagine in your hand is a chocolate heart, covered with shiny red or silver foil. When you see the wrapped candy, you realize that, to get to the chocolate, you have to peel away the wrapping. What a good reminder of real-life relationships! You often have to peel away the outside layers to get to the core of who you are. When people are too concerned with the shiny outside, they may fail to look inside and discover who they are or who the other person is. The really good stuff is inside; yet, if you spend too much time arranging and rearranging the outside, you may not *get* to the inside.

> It is only with the heart that one can see rightly; what is essential is invisible to the eye.
>
> — *Antoine de Saint Exupery*

A few years ago, I was asked to host a show on which I interviewed women who had elective plastic surgery. The two women were lovely with their new faces. I was interested to see the outer transformation but much more interested in discussing whether the procedure changed how they felt. For both women, the nips and tucks had made them value themselves more because they felt younger and more attractive, but it hadn't changed who they were inside.

> There is only one journey, going inside yourself.
>
> – *Rainer Maria Rilke*

Our society is eager to do makeovers—television shows like *The Biggest Loser*, *The Swan*, *Nip/Tuck*, even Dr. Phil and Oprah are in on the act. All these shows imply that we need to fix the outside to be able to feel good on the inside. The therapist in me thinks it's the other way around. Fix the inside, and the outside will shine.

The late humorist Sam Levinson wrote a poem about beauty that became a favorite of Audrey Hepburn. The poem begins, "The beauty of a woman is not in the clothes she wears, the figure she carries, or the way she combs her hair. The beauty of a woman must be seen in her eyes because that is the doorway to her heart, the place where love resides . . . "

> What lies behind you and what lies before you are tiny matters compared to what lies within you.
>
> – *Emerson*

There's a wonderful story of a Sufi named Malfi, who had lost his house key. He was crawling around outside looking for his key when a friend came by. After helping Malfi to look for a while, his friend asked, "Where did you lose the key?"

Malfi replied, "Inside the house."

"Then why are we looking for it out here?"

"Because there's more light out here," said Malfi.

It's true that sometimes it is dark inside ourselves. You may have to look at traits you have hidden for a long time—your shadow self. To look at these traits and take an honest self-inventory is not an easy task. You have blind spots and are unable to see in the dark recesses of your soul.

Living is an inside job, and sometimes journeying onward is done alone, in solitude, on retreats or vision quests. Dan Millman, in his book, *The Laws of Spirit*, tells us, "Look inside, listen to the outside, but be guided by the wisdom of the heart." Good advice.

It's easier to look at the outside than it is to go inside and look at yourselves or others, but the only lasting and important ingredients are within. Let the chocolate heart remind you that your heart has eyes. So look with your heart and feelings to uncover the core self, because it is what's inside that counts. Unwrap the foil and dig in.

# Activities for Unwrapping the Foil

1. **Write a personal ad.** ✍

   Imagine you are writing an ad in search of a best friend. Describe the inner qualities you'd like him or her to have.

2. **Describe yourself.** 📄

   List five qualities that are your foil wrapping outside and five that represent the sweet chocolate inside.

3. **Make contact.** 📧

   Call or send a card to a friend, spouse, or child, and tell them why you appreciate them. Describe their inner sweetness.

4. **Draw yourself.** ✏

   Sketch a picture of your outer, physical self—what people see when they first meet you. Then draw your inner self—what people don't see immediately. Now look at the two pictures and decide if there's a part of your inner self that you'd like to show others more readily. Here's your opportunity to change.

5. **Leave the familiar.** 🌲

   Go on a retreat or spiritual adventure. Go alone or with a friend. Omega Institute in Rhinebeck, N.Y., has many spiritual programs. You can check their website for current programs at www.eomega.org.

# A Chocolate Heart Reminds Us:

- To savor the flavor of chocolate

- To share caring contact and connection

- To create passion

- To look inside ourselves and others

Describe in your journal what a chocolate heart symbolizes to you.

*SYMBOL THREE*

# An Elastic Band

# CHAPTER 10

# An Elastic Band

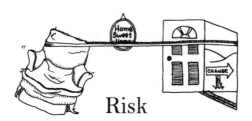

## Risk

An elastic band is a tiny item, capable of being stretched or expanded. Sometimes it takes only a minor pull for the elastic band to change. At other times we need to really tug to get the band the size we want. Just like an elastic band, we need to stretch ourselves by being open to both change and appropriate risk-taking in our lives.

Often we need some pressure exerted on us before we will risk growth or expansion. In fact, because we are resistant to change, most of the time many of us would prefer to sit in our easy chair and stay exactly as we are.

> And the day came when the risk to remain tight in the bud became more painful than the risk it took to blossom.
>
> — Anais Nin

"There are only two things in life that we can be sure of," according to author Dr. Leo Buscaglia, "death and change, and we don't like either very much." Only when we expand, grow, and take some risks do we increase our awareness and raise our self-esteem. We then find ourselves enjoying new areas of life and walking down new streets.

When an elastic band is pulled, there's inherent tension. When outside pressures prompt us to change, we may feel anxious. Perhaps you have a baby on the way, and you need to change jobs to make ends meet. It can be difficult learning to live with this tension and find balance. Balance is the key ingredient to risk-taking. We want to embrace change, but we don't want to stretch beyond our capabilities and snap apart like a dry, old rubber band.

> One can never consent to creep when one feels an impulse to soar.
>
> — *Helen Keller*

When I talk about risk, many of my clients assume I'm talking only about dangerous, physical risks, such as bungee jumping or mountain climbing. Appropriate physical risk might actually be of interest to you. Perhaps you want to learn to ski or take a spinning class at a local gym. If so, that's great. Understand, however, that risk-taking can also be emotional, intellectual, financial, or spiritual.

An emotional risk might be telling a person, for the first time, that you love him or her. An intellectual risk may be taking a class in the philosophy of the ancient Greeks. A spiritual risk could be going to a weekend meditation retreat. A financial risk might be a first-time stock market investment or starting your own business.

Many of the most successful entrepreneurs and millionaires have been bankrupt numerous times. They continued to risk. Walt Disney went bankrupt five times and was never able to raise the money for Epcot Center. Yet he continued to risk and follow his dream, and today his legacy enriches millions of lives.

The type of risk we are inclined to take often varies with our gender and our personality. For example, after a death in the family, a woman is more likely to share her emotions about the loss than is a man. An extrovert is more inclined to talk to strangers than is an introvert.

The process of planned risk-taking, however, is similar for everyone. First, acknowledge that you want to change. Next, make a decision to take an appropriate risk. Third, make a plan, identify alternatives, and consider consequences. Finally, act and follow through with perseverance.

> All things are possible until they are proven impossible — and even the impossible may only be so as of now.
>
> — *Pearl S. Buck*

I moved to Florida in 1990 and didn't know a single person. My dream was to start my own private marriage-and-family practice.

People said, "Are you crazy? You don't know anyone. You have no contacts."

I said, "It's my dream. I want to follow my dream."

For over twenty years, I had been a teacher and guidance counselor in public schools. I always worked for someone else but received a steady paycheck.

I was risking a lot—no salary, no benefits, no support system. It was one of the most frightening and exciting times of my life. I stretched out of my comfort zone in all areas—emotional, financial, intellectual, spiritual, and physical. "Sometimes you just have to jump and grow your wings on the way down." I painted that quote on my office wall to remind both my clients and me of the importance of risk-taking. Today, after years of hard work and risk-taking, I am blessed with a wonderful, successful counseling practice. I jumped and learned to fly.

> Do one thing every day that scares you.
>
> — *Eleanor Roosevelt*

I invite you to expand your comfort zone. Once you take a risk in one area, and you're successful, it's easier to take on a challenge in another part of your life.

Once the elastic band stretches, it may look the same, but it never returns to exactly the same size. It is changed forever. We, too, are changed forever every time we take a risk.

The elasticity of the rubber band reminds us to be open and to expand into calculated risks. It reminds us to face fear and just do it. Fear is the greatest enemy of change and risk-taking. Anthony de Mello, in *The Heart of the Enlightened*, tells the following parable of Pestilence speeding to Damascus on his way to kill a thousand people.

Upon leaving town, he was stopped and asked, "Why did you kill fifty thousand? You said you were taking only a thousand." Pestilence replied, "I took only a thousand. Fear took the rest."

> Soar, eat ether, see what has never been seen; depart, be lost, but climb.
>
> — *Edna St. Vincent Millay*

It is often our fear that stops us from seeing our options. F.E.A.R. is **F**orgetting **E**verything is **A**ll **R**ight. It takes courage to break out of the FEAR trap. The word "courage" comes from the Greek word for *heart*, "cœur." Take heart (courage) and risk changing.

# Activities for Developing Appropriate Risk-Taking

## 1. **Begin the process.** ➲

Think of your present life and situation. Can you think of an area in which you need to be open to taking a risk? What can you do *today* to expand yourself? Use this four-step process for risk-taking:

Step 1: Identify what needs to be changed.

> *I'm going to die on the vine if I stay in this job.*

Step 2: Make the decision to take a risk, and *write it down.*

> *I will actively seek and find a better paying job that I enjoy.*
>
> *I enjoy x, y, and z.*

Step 3: Make a plan.

> *I will:*
>
> - *Send out letters to friends*
> - *Go to the library and research job opportunities*
> - *Read the classified ads*
> - *Take a course on career development*

Step 4: Act and follow through. Take baby steps. If you run into a wall, continue to take baby steps in a parallel direction.

## 2. **Create a risk chart.** ✎

Copy the chart on the next page and fill it in with six things you love to do. Check the appropriate column to indicate which category of risk is stretched when you participate in each activity.

| Activity | Physical | Emotional | Intellectual | Spiritual | Financial |
|---|---|---|---|---|---|
| ♦ Tennis | ✓ | | | | |
| ♦ Study Spanish | | | ✓ | | |
| ♦ Take Meditation Class | | | | ✓ | |
| ♦ Invest in Stock Market | | | | | ✓ |
| ♦ Therapy/Counseling | | ✓ | | | |

*Example: Maybe one of the things you love to do is play tennis, and that's a physical risk for you. By risk, I don't mean dangerous to your health, I mean challenging. Perhaps most of the things you enjoy fall under the physical and intellectual risk categories, so you may need to take more emotional, spiritual, or financial risks.*

## 3. Take small, new risks. ?

Engage in a few small risks outside of your priority area. Do one thing differently today. Listen to new music, and really listen to the tone and the words. Wear different color clothes, or put on clothes you have never worn together. Go for a walk in a new place. Take the scenic route to work. Talk to the person in the elevator, the bank, or the grocery checkout line. Try your hair parted in a different place, or wear your hair in a new style. Go to a lecture on something about which you know nothing.

# CHAPTER 11

# An Elastic Band

## Resiliency

An elastic band is a symbol of our resiliency, our ability to bounce back, to bend and not break. The willow tree bends and sways in a storm, whereas the rigid oak may snap in half if the winds are too strong.

We all stumble in life. The challenge is to pick ourselves up, brush off the dirt, and come out of the fall with only minor injuries. We learn to take another street. Obstacles and problems in life often force us to transcend pain, suffering, frustrations, or loss, so we may survive, flourish, and reach our goals.

The anonymous poem on the next page, "Autobiography in Five Short Chapters," speaks to the feelings many of us share about change and our resilient nature.

Much research has been done on resilient individuals, which has helped to turn the focus of psychology away from what causes damage to people (a victim model), and toward an attempt to understand

### AUTOBIOGRAPHY IN FIVE SHORT CHAPTERS

**CHAPTER I**

I walk down the street.
    There is a deep hole in the sidewalk.
I fall in.
        I am lost . . . I am helpless.
          It isn't my fault.
It takes forever to find my way out.

**CHAPTER II**

I walk down the same street.
    There is a deep hole in the sidewalk.
    I pretend I don't see it.
    I fall in again.
        I can't believe I'm in the same place,
          but it isn't my fault.
It still takes a long time to find my way out.

**CHAPTER III**

I walk down the same street.
    There is a deep hole in the sidewalk.
    I see it there.
I still fall in . . . it's a habit.
        My eyes are open.
        I know where I am.
          It's my fault.
        I get out immediately.

**CHAPTER IV**

I walk down the same street.
    There is a deep hole in the sidewalk.
    I walk around it.

**CHAPTER V**

I walk down another street.

what makes them strong (a healthy model).

The Chinese symbol for crisis is a combination of two symbols: one is opportunity and the other is growth. In the summer of 2001, my daughter and I went to China for a month. We took a Yangtze River cruise, one of the last before the dam was completed and the river was allowed to flood hundreds of villages. Villages that existed for thousands of years would be flooded! The government planned to relocate millions of people, moving them up the side of the mountain to higher ground and reestablishing their villages there. My daughter and I were amazed at the positive attitude and resiliency of some of the villagers we met. They truly seemed to view this crisis as an opportunity for growth.

How many of us could do the same?

In 2004, many people had the opportunity to view crisis as an opportunity for growth. Thousands of people in Florida survived four hurricanes and rebuilt their lives. A tsunami in Asia took the lives of hundreds of thousands. In 2005, hundreds of thousands relocated after Hurricane Katrina. Still, the human spirit rebounds. It is truly amazing.

> For a righteous man falls seven times, and rises again.
>
> — *Proverbs 24:16*

Psychologist Sybil Wolin, Ph.D., and her husband, psychiatrist Steve Wolin, M.D., co-authored the popular book, *The Resilient Self*. The Wolins have identified six qualities of resilient people: insight, humor, independence, initiative, creativity, and morality. In their work, the Wolins encourage individuals to discover their "Survivor's Pride," which means to reframe the way they see themselves. People learn to acknowledge their strengths as well as the coping skills they develop during the rough times.

Other research supports the finding that resilient people share common traits.

- They have a basic belief in their ability to set goals and to change.
- They recognize their strengths and see themselves as strategists.
- They have an ability to perceive bad times as temporary and have faith in the future or a higher power.
- They see failure as a friend and try to learn from it.
- They take action to reduce their fear and try not to go it alone.

- The most important characteristic of resilient people is the ability to create or expand their circle of support, even if they didn't start out in a loving environment.

One of the most interesting outcomes of this research is that experts now believe resiliency isn't only innate but can be learned.

Every day I work with my clients helping them learn or relearn some of these resilient traits. Many years ago I had a client who was fearful of being on her own. Although she was married to an abusive alcoholic, she believed it was better than being alone. As we explored her childhood, she told me a story that haunts me today, twenty years later. When she was a three-month-old baby, her parents left her with a babysitter and went away for the weekend. While bathing her, the sitter had a heart attack and died immediately. This little baby lay alone in the bathtub all weekend until her parents returned Sunday night. No wonder she is afraid of being alone! In therapy she learned to navigate the waters of her life and stand up for herself. She was able to venture out into safer water (relationships), knowing she was a survivor.

> Never give in, never give in, never, never, never...
>
> —*Winston Churchill*

The elasticity of the rubber band reminds us to be flexible and that we can learn to bounce back from a trauma. An elastic band is shaped like a circle that can be expanded. This reminds us to expand our circle of friends and mentors so we can support one another in realizing our dreams.

# Activities for Developing Resiliency

## 1. Take a resiliency inventory. ☑

Think of your life in blocks of five years. Jot down names of people who influenced you during those years, significant positive events (a great college experience) or challenging situations (losing a job). Certain time frames may have more than one event. Add as many as you like. Note the most growth-producing time(s) in your life.

$$0\text{----------}5\text{----------}10\text{----------}15\text{----------}20\text{----------}$$
$$25\text{----------}30\text{----------}35\text{----------}40\text{----------}45\text{----------}$$
$$50\text{----------}55\text{----------}60\text{----------}65\text{----------}70\text{----------}$$
$$75\text{----------}80\text{----------}85\text{----------}90\text{----------}95\text{----------}$$

Which of the following resiliency traits did you use to bounce back during the rough times?

| Insight | Humor | Creativity |
|---|---|---|
| Independence | Initiative | Morality |

## 2. Describe a past event. ✍

Think of a situation when you were resilient. Then write which resiliency traits you used to recover.

*Example: (author's personal story) When I was visiting Washington, D.C., my luggage was stolen from my rental car. I had just been to the Holocaust Museum and realized that the inconvenience of being robbed was nothing compared to what happened to the people in the concentration camps (insight). The good news was that I didn't have to get in the luggage line at the airport, and I got to buy all new clothes (humor). I temporarily fixed the broken window using borrowed cardboard and masking tape so I could drive the car in the rain (creativity).*

# CHAPTER 12

# An Elastic Band

## Stretch

The way an elastic band stretches symbolizes the importance of physical motion for a healthy body and mind. Doctors tell us that regular exercise does more than just combat fat and bad cholesterol. It can lift our moods. We can also view exercise as a first-line treatment for depression.

I used to facilitate a depression support group for our local mental health association. Every week we began the meetings with gentle stretches, reaching for the sky, bending and touching the earth at our toes, and then opening up our diaphragms and chests with arm stretches out from our sides. The participants often joked that the session was more like an exercise class than a depression support group. But they soon began stretching on their own as part of their daily rituals and found that their depression lessened.

Emotional support, stretching, and medication might all be necessary to help cure depression. Drugs may help a depressed person feel functional, but exercise helps a person feel vibrant.

When I lecture, one of my audience participation routines goes like this:

"Try it with me now. Stand up and bend at the waist. Look at your feet and say, 'I'm happy,' three times out loud.

"Now stand up straight. Reach toward the sky. Look up. March in place. Raise one arm above your head, then the other, reaching for the stars. Say, 'I'm depressed,' as you march in place, looking up and reaching for the stars. Do this three times, too. It is almost impossible to be sad when your diaphragm is open and the energy is moving through your body."

Doctors are now handing out written prescriptions that instruct their patients to start an exercise regime. If you have couch-potato tendencies, then exercise regularly with a friend or join a class. Just as an elastic band holds things together, when we have an exercise buddy it helps us hold our commitment together.

Our society is becoming increasingly technological and, as a result, more sedentary. Yet stretching, exercising, and breathing are essential to keep the brain functioning efficiently. The brain needs one quarter of your body's total fuel supply. It also needs oxygen. You can get a quick boost by yawning a few times or breathing deeply.

> Stimulated by exercise, our life-flame burns with a clearer ray, and we are charged with the joy of being wholly alive.
>
> — *Gene Tunney*

My work as a therapist is quite sedentary. I often sit for eight or nine hours a day with only five-minute breaks between each session. This lifestyle caught up with me when I entered menopause. I found myself in one of the deepest depressions I had ever experienced. I was almost immobile. In a desperate attempt to feel better, I joined a health club and began to work out. I dragged myself to the club first thing in the morning, got on the treadmill or bike, and began lifting weights and stretching. I'm not going to say that I breezed through menopause, but at least I *breathed* through it with more serenity, lightness, and control.

Now I awake at 5:15 a.m. three days a week and go to a 6:00 a.m. aerobics class. The exercise to music in a dark room starts my day in a fun way. Something about the energy from the class gives me a lift. We begin and end with stretches. Stretching is essential to keep you flexible. Stretches should be gentle and slow. The goal is to ease the tension in tight muscles and work toward a flexible body. Part of any exercise routine should involve stretching. You can do stretches anytime, anywhere, and stay flexible. Try it; you'll like it!

An elastic band reminds us to stretch, exercise, and breathe for mental and physical health.

# Activities for Stretching the Body

1. **Exercise regularly.**

   Find a partner and exercise together. This could be a personal trainer, a neighbor, a class, a group of runners, a dog, or a baby in a stroller. Make a plan to exercise for at least thirty minutes, three to four times per week.

2. **Take a yoga class.**

   Buy or rent a yoga tape/DVD; many excellent videos are available.

3. **Stretch frequently.**

   Stand up and reach for the sky, feel your vertebrae open up, bend forward and let your arms and neck dangle, and relax into the stretch. If you're like me and can't touch your toes, don't strain; just feel the stretch. Bend from side to side.

4. **Remember to breathe.**

   Most people's breathing becomes very shallow or even stops briefly when they are scared or anxious. Take a deep breath in through your nose, hold for the count of five, and slowly blow the breath out through your mouth like you're blowing bubbles. Repeat this three times, and you will feel calmer.

5. **Expand your lungs.**

   Yawn deliberately a few times every hour.

# An Elastic Band Reminds Us:

- To expand our comfort zone

- That we can snap back into place

- To exercise and breathe

Describe in your journal what a rubber band symbolizes to you.

# A Pencil

# CHAPTER 13

# A Pencil

## Written Communication

A pencil is a basic tool of written communication—a slender, rod-shaped, wooden instrument with a core of graphite. It is a light, economical, and dependable tool. Pencils work by manual control—the only energy source you need is your own movement. There is no need to worry about power surges, your computer freezing, or accidentally hitting the delete button and losing your work. You are in complete control of the output. A pencil is the middleman for the translation of an idea from thought to written reality.

> Writing is an exploration. You start from nothing and learn as you go.
>
> *— E.L. Doctorow*

The pencil helps us share our thoughts in a more permanent form through writing. When we see our words on paper, they come to life. Writing is a tangible, personal representation of who we are. It is a means of experiencing life and expressing emotions, notions, entertainment, and facts—as well as documenting history. We can be as elaborate or as simple as we choose in sharing our message, just by using a pencil to do the job.

When you first learned to write, you may have received a diary as a gift. The diary, or journal, is one of the primary tools I recommend to my clients to help them discover their personal wisdom, actualize their dreams, and release their demons. Here are some tips for keeping a journal:

> Writing is like running: the more you do it, the better you get at it.
>
> — *Natalie Goldberg*

Many times my clients say, "I'm not in the mood to write today." Put yourself in the mood. Try closing your eyes and taking five deep breaths. This clears your mind from the day and focuses you inward. Think, "What am I feeling right now?" Describe the feeling.

You can also jot down a few lines to summarize the high or low points of your day. Often a quotation, topic, or question can be a good starting point in your journal writing. What does today's quotation mean to me? Why did I notice this today? Sometimes creating dialogues helps add a new dimension to our writing. I've also seen great personal discoveries come from writing that explores roads not taken in life. Descriptors that fast-forward our lives one month or one year can provide valuable insight. Be as descriptive as possible; it helps your brain now and in the future.

Many years ago, I had a deeply troubled family in therapy. Two teenage children were diagnosed with bipolar disorder, the family had serious financial problems, and the husband was having an affair. The overprotective mother felt desperate as she watched her family disintegrate and her life spin out of control. She searched for a way to stay connected to her children.

Because she loved writing, she kept a journal in which she wrote letters to her daughters and in which she invited them to reply. This mother/daughter journal became a valued treasure. They wrote about their fears, hopes, and dreams—a little of everything. Sometimes they just talked about silly things, crazy conversations, or their favorite foods. The journal helped them to weather the storm together. It was a safe haven for learning about themselves and one another.

> Finally, one just has to shut up, sit down, and write.
>
> — *Natalie Goldberg*

Their dialogue became a precursor to healthy action, and now their relationship is stronger than ever. I have also seen couples use this technique to improve their relationships. Marriage enrichment programs employ letter-writing to develop or rekindle intimacy and emotional connection. Writing increases commitment and says, "This marriage is important, and I'm taking the time to write and prove it!"

Writing helps to forge a link between your heart and mind—just what a relationship needs. The permanent nature of the written word helps both to clarify the issues between people and to lessen the chance of miscommunication. This is why contracts exist. Writing doesn't have "tone" the way that speaking does. What you see is exactly what you get.

Any and all forms of written communication are vital for healthy relationships. So send letters, postcards, e-mail, faxes, or cards for any reason or occasion. Write it down, drop a line, say, "Hello, just thinking of you," or "Thank you." Say it in writing; it "sounds" louder, and it lasts longer.

When my daughter left for college, I vowed to do something meaningful to stay connected with her. I bought dozens of postcards and sent them almost daily. Most of them simply said, "Love you, miss you, are you studying?" or "Hang in there." The cards now provide a sweet memoir of her college years, and they strengthened our bond.

Be sure to use the pencil as a tool to help you, not to make your life more encumbered and stressful. "To do" lists are great for organizing your life, but it's easy to become a slave to them. Too often I see people who are stressed out because they feel they will never get everything done. They focus on the things left "to do" on the list, rather than on the positive "I did it!" list. Look often at what you *have accomplished*, not just at what remains to be done.

We all have pencils lying around our home, school, or office. They serve as reminders that the written word is a fundamental form of communication and that the simple pencil is a magnificent tool.

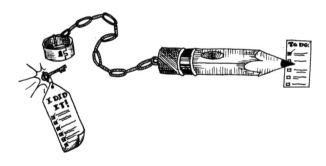

# Activities for Enlivening Written Communication

*For all of these activities, please write by hand, preferably with a pencil. We use more motor skills when we write by hand than when we type. This helps us access our emotions to a greater degree.*

1. **Start a personal journal.** 📖

   Journal writing is an important growth experience. In *The Artist's Way*, author Julia Cameron suggests writing three longhand pages every morning as soon as you arise. This pencil-to-paper technique will help you capture the dream state and awaken your creativity. It can also facilitate "brain drain," a sense of just letting out the concern and worries of the day or night.

   *Example: "This morning my body aches, it's so hard to move. I know that I need to get to the gym, because only then can I get the blood flowing again. How I hate this feeling! Have to call Kirsten and see if the chair got delivered and if she likes it. Hope it goes in her dorm and fits under the loft. She sounded so sad the last few times we talked. I know it's hard for her to adjust to college and dorm life. Maybe she should have gone closer to home, twelve hours is such a long way away..."*

2. **Start scripting.** ✏️

   Scripting is a wishful writing technique that re-trains your unconscious and helps you create your future. Write all the dreams and hopes you have in the present tense, as if they were already happening. Create your vision in writing. Do this once a month, then set it aside. Reread it weekly and make any updates or changes. Focus on the positive.

*Example: "I am really finding satisfaction in my work. I'm using my creativity and teaching skills to help my clients.* Everyday Symbols for Joyful Living *has received national recognition. Book sales are over the top—a new 'Chicken Soup.' I am scheduled for bi-monthly speaking engagements across the country. Karla and Kelly are excited about the accolades and financial abundance we are all reaping. It's a great time!"*

3. **Start a shared journal.**

It can be a two-way, three-way, or family journal.

4. **Create an "I did it!" list.**

At the end of the day, write down everything you accomplished during the day. The "I did it!" list focuses on the positive. We learn self-validation for work accomplished rather than self-criticism for what remains on the endless "To do" list.

# CHAPTER 14

# A Pencil

## Emotional Release

Have you ever broken a pencil in two while in a rage? Just snapping the pencil makes you feel better. Researchers have found that writing, not just breaking the pencil, can be a healthy way to release anger because it can actually lower blood pressure. Wouldn't it be great if the drug companies gave out writing journals with their high blood pressure medication?

Why do we have so much pent-up anger? Take a look at babies. They cry, laugh, smile, and move their arms and legs. Infants automatically release feelings through these channels. When we grow up, we learn to censor our expression of emotion, especially the emotions society considers "unpleasant" or "negative." We contain these emotions until the container overflows and they come bursting out in inappropriate ways. Feelings aren't negative or positive; it's the expression of them that can be perceived as good or bad.

Emotions fall into four primary categories: mad, sad, glad, and scared. All of them need to be released; but most of us are better at releasing glad or happy feelings than we are at releasing angry, sad, and fearful ones.

Dealing with anger and letting go of pain are two major problems for society today. One need only look at the newspaper or the evening news for proof of that. In addition to being a social problem, anger can exacerbate many health problems, such as high blood pressure, ulcers, and cancer. Learning sound ways to release our anger will improve not only our health but our financial situation, as well, because we won't need to visit the doctor as often.

> Men with clenched fists cannot shake hands.
>
> — *Sufi Teaching*

Anger is a powerful energy and emotion, but many appropriate ways exist to release it. Walk around, run up and down stairs, become the office shredding machine—rip paper into tiny pieces—jog in place like Rocky Balboa. All these physical activities can help release anger. One non-physical tool that is often forgotten, however, is writing.

As a therapy assignment, I have suggested that clients write letters to parents, spouses, ex-spouses, children, friends, ex-friends, partners, sexual abusers, and even aborted fetuses. Some clients were in tears during the exercise because the writing evoked horrid memories of trauma. The letters were read aloud to me and then buried, burned, or ripped up and flushed away. Please note, however, that a handwritten letter to blow off steam or release pain facilitates the healing process, but it should **not** be sent.

The pencil can also be used to discuss issues and solve problems too emotionally charged or toxic to talk about in person. Putting pencil to paper helps us to clarify our ideas and points, making it easier for us to understand ourselves and others. Writing can create a rational form of communication in the heat of a very irrational time.

Unresolved anger is certainly a major issue in relationships. It builds walls between people—walls that are created one angry brick at a time. I teach families to take a "writing timeout." This means they walk away from the person with whom they are in conflict, grab a pencil, and write down their rage and aggravation. Anger, after all, is only agitated energy. Writing is such a healthy way to release this energy.

> Consider how much more often you suffer from your anger and grief, than from those very things for which you are angry and grieved.
>
> — *Marcus Aurelius*

Here's the trick: write, read what you have written, and then set it aside. When you have cooled off, reread it and decide what you want to do with it—bury it, crumple it, save it, burn it, or edit it to be constructive so you can share it with the relevant person.

Remember, receiving a letter full of irrational rantings is very unpleasant, and does **not** pave the way to clear communication. Such letters hurt feelings and place addressees on the defensive, causing them to be in "reaction mode," instead of an open, receptive, and aware state. Use the pencil as a tool to release "negative" painful emotions, but be careful not to inflict them on anyone else. Do it "write."

# Activities for Releasing Emotions

1. **Free associate.**

   Write the word ANGER at the top of the page. Think of all the things you are angry about, or the people with whom you are angry. Just start writing, and write it all out—no censoring. Let out all the rage and garbage. Then tear up the paper and take it to the trash. Think or visualize that the anger is being released. Repeat this activity with SAD and AFRAID.

2. **Write yourself an apology.**

   Think of a person who has hurt you, and write an apology letter *from* that person to you. Get into the other person's shoes, then write everything you need to hear in order to forgive them. You know what you need to hear, so say it in writing to yourself. Read the letter out loud to a friend or to yourself. Let yourself hear it and accept it. Then move on.

3. **Write a letter to someone who has hurt you.**

   Explain your pain and how their behavior has affected you. Be as specific as possible. *Do not mail the letter.* Keep it a day or two, reread it, and revise it. Face an empty chair and pretend that the person with whom you are angry is sitting there. Read the letter. Say everything you'd like to tell them—UNCENSORED. Yell if you feel like it. Then tear it up, burn it, or bury it. Imagine letting go of the pain or rage. If you think of the pain again, remember how you let go of it once, and keep your intent to do so again.

## 4. **Put conflicts on paper.** 🗐

As an alternative to arguing with someone, agree to commit all toxic exchanges to paper. Take a writing timeout during a conflict, and each of you write out your thoughts. Then exchange letters and respond. If no agreement can be reached, agree to disagree.

## 5. **Make a comfort list.** 📖

Copy the list below into your journal and cross out all the feelings with which you're comfortable. Circle all the feelings that make you uncomfortable. This week, focus on one of the circled words and see if you can feel easier with that emotion. This will help you to identify feelings without judgment.

| | | |
|---|---|---|
| • Aggressive | • Fearful | • Peaceful |
| • Alienated | • Glad | • Proud |
| • Angry | • Guilty | • Regretful |
| • Anxious | • Helpless | • Relieved |
| • Confident | • Hopeful | • Sad |
| • Curious | • Hostile | • Satisfied |
| • Depressed | • Humiliated | • Scared |
| • Determined | • Lonely | • Shy |
| • Discouraged | • Loved | • Sorry |
| • Embarrassed | • Mad | • Stubborn |
| • Enthusiastic | • Mischievous | • Suspicious |
| • Envious | • Optimistic | • Undecided |
| • Excited | • Paranoid | • Withdrawn |

# CHAPTER 15

# A Pencil

## Erase It

A pencil with an eraser on top symbolizes the need to take responsibility for our mistakes and to apologize so we can mend the mistakes we've made. We also need to forgive ourselves and others for making mistakes, and then move on. Dwelling on mistakes serves no purpose.

As kids we often used up the eraser first. We felt free to make use of it and start over. In fact, we could buy another eraser, pop it on our pencil, and get back to work. Most adults rarely use an eraser. Perhaps this symbolizes our view of mistakes, our inability to admit to them and try again.

> Write injuries
> in dust,
> benefits in marble.
>
> *— Benjamin Franklin*

"Love means never having to say you're sorry," was a naïve message from the 1970s movie *Love Story*. Real life and real love can be messy at times. It is a dangerous illusion to think that true romantic love can continue indefinitely with no struggle and no conflict. Loving relationships are hard work, and people who live together can drive each other crazy over the trivial matters involved in sharing the same space—let alone the same bed. Close proximity makes us vulnerable. The person closest to us knows us the best and can hurt us the most. That person may be the one who receives the brunt of our anger, even if he or she had nothing to do with the rotten day we had at work or school.

It's easy to erase what is written; it takes just a flick of the wrist. With a little practice, it's also easy to say the two little words, "I'm sorry," and to ask for forgiveness from others and ourselves. An apology says, "I'm big enough to admit that I was wrong, and I care enough to tell you." An apology opens the receiver's heart and facilitates forgiveness.

Forgiveness is a complex process. The first step is to decide that we want and need to forgive. The forgiveness journey takes time and can often be a difficult, painful, winding path. It involves letting go and forgetting revenge. The reason for the forgiveness journey is simple and actually selfish. We need to forgive because carrying the hurt controls our lives and weighs us down. Forgiveness frees us and lightens our emotional baggage.

> If we really want to love,
> we must learn to forgive.
>
> — *Mother Teresa*

Imagine that you are carrying a sturdy backpack. Every time someone hurts you—and you can't forgive them—imagine that a potato is being placed in the backpack. Big hurts, big potatoes. Little hurts, little potatoes. As time goes on, the pack gets heavier, and then it starts to stink. Forgiveness means you can let go of the old, smelly potatoes and continue briskly on your life's journey.

Forgiveness is a process made easier with words and actions. Use both because actions speak as loudly as words.

Being able to forgive is essential for healthy living. Forgiving releases the hurt and anger that have controlled our lives and thoughts. It is hard work to forgive emotional injuries, and it may take longer than you think. Remember, the willingness to forgive takes courage and strength. Give yourself permission to forgive.

> It is easier to forgive an enemy than to forgive a friend.
>
> — *William Blake*

Some things feel too atrocious to forgive. If you feel you can't yet forgive, or if the person hasn't asked for forgiveness, just allow yourself to be open to the possibility. It will be worth it, because in bestowing the gift of forgiveness, we are healed and freed from bondage.

A pencil with an eraser reminds us that love means *being able* to say, "I'm sorry." It reminds us to accept the apologies of others and to forgive them.

# Activities for Erasing
# Mistakes and Moving on

### 1. Write an apology. ✏️

Is there someone to whom you owe an apology? Find a card, write a short letter, or make a phone call, and say, "I'm sorry." Be specific about what you are sorry for, and indicate a changed action you will take from now on. A good formula for an apology is: (Name), I'm sorry for (action that offended). I will try to (corrective action).

*Example: "John, I'm sorry for calling you an inconsiderate idiot. I won't call you names in the future. If I disagree with the way you're doing things, I'll find a constructive, clear way to communicate my feelings."*

### 2. Watch yourself as you apologize. 👁️

Look in the mirror and practice saying, "I'm sorry." See how you look. Try it on. Say, "I'm sorry" to yourself. Notice how it looks and feels to be compassionate and forgiving of yourself, then describe it in your journal. Be as specific as possible.

### 3. Create a forgiveness list. 📄

Make a list of things for which you need to forgive yourself. Write yourself an apology. Put it in an envelope and save it. When you feel angry with yourself, take it out and reread it.

*Example: Dear Dianne, I'm sorry for not teaching you how to handle rage and anger. I know you aren't able to express your anger, and I hope you will learn to state directly what gets you upset instead of stuffing it down with comfort foods.    Love, Dianne*

## 4. Employ visualization techniques. 🗩

If you are upset with someone you can't yet forgive, try this activity. Use a deep breathing technique to achieve a fully relaxed state. Imagine yourself talking with the people who hurt you. Visualize them as being truly contrite. In your mind's eye, see them apologize sincerely. Allow yourself to experience how good it feels to accept their apology. Do this daily—many times each day. See it and feel it. The more times you do it, the better. Notice how you begin to feel. Letting go may be your gift for this activity.

## 5. Apologize for mistakes. 👄

Apologize when you make a mistake during the next twenty-eight days. It takes at least twenty-eight days to begin to change a habit. Make this a new habit.

# A Pencil Reminds Us:

- To share our thoughts and feelings on paper

- To address our feelings and let them go

- To say that we're sorry and to forgive

Please use your journal to describe what a pencil symbolizes to you.

*SYMBOL FIVE*

# A Crayon

# CHAPTER 16

# A Crayon
## Play

A crayon reminds us of ourselves in childhood—perhaps kindergarten or first grade—as we created our first picture in a coloring book. That happy, carefree child still lives within each of us. A crayon is the symbol that reminds us to play, and play is children's work. It is one of those things that may seem superficial, like a waste of time, but we can't live well without it.

As we age, we tend to take play for granted until it no longer exists in our lives. Then our lives lack color, passion, and fun. Play is much like breathing; it is done effortlessly. It can't be forced, or it will feel like a task. It arises naturally out of a relaxed state.

The trick to recapturing our inner child is to allow time and a relaxed space for this important ingredient—play—in our lives. Don't let "scare city" get in your way. Do an "a bun dance" and enjoy.

> Carpe diem.
>
> – Horace

Observe and hold a crayon, then think of the times in your life that have been the most playful. How do you play? When do you play? Birth order, as well as personality, impacts our view of play. Some people, especially if they are the youngest in their family, seem to find it easier to play. They are the ones who have crayons or a set of colored markers stashed in a drawer, or who are always telling jokes or playing tricks on others.

I am a firstborn who viewed life very seriously and considered play too frivolous an activity for adults. Yet I knew that play was important for kids, so when my daughter was born I "imported" a good friend—an adult who was the baby in his own family—and he romped with my daughter on the floor and tossed her up into the air. He knew how to be goofy. I learned from him how to add playfulness to my daughter's life and how to add it to my own. Now, when I go to a restaurant that has crayons and paper tablecloths, I dive right into creating a fantasy drawing. If a string quartet comes to serenade my dinner table, I sing along.

> You're only here for a short visit. Don't hurry. Don't worry. And be sure to smell the flowers along the way.
>
> — *Walter Hagen*

Recently, I was invited to participate in a fantastically fun experience. As a fundraiser for one of our local private schools, an auction item was created by a very creative and playful mom. "Never Fake It Again" parties were auctioned off. Participants paid one thousand dollars each to attend three parties. The first was "Never Fake Your Artistic Ability," at which a local artist helped the group dabble in mosaic art. The second party was "Never Fake Your Football Knowledge," and the wife of a Miami Dolphin came and shared her knowledge of football plays. The third, "Never Fake Your Serenity," was my day. We took a boat to a private island where everyone received "serenity bags" filled with goodies—sand pail and sand toys, a magic wand, bubbles, worry dolls, my book and journal, a happy face light-up pen, and a month of inspirational messages. We floated in the sea, made sand angels and sand castles, read inspirational messages and books, and created a magical fantasy for a day. Everyone went home with their own "symbols of serenity" bag to help them remember to bring playfulness, joy, and serenity into their daily lives.

I also keep a *Magic Mandala Coloring Book* in my waiting room. This book was created by Martha Bartfeld, an eighty-year-young lady from New Mexico. Mandalas are abstract, geometric shapes—typically found in the Buddhist religion—that are symbolic of the universe and that aid in meditation. My clients—children and adults of all ages—create beautiful mandalas with colored pencils or crayons as they wait. I am impressed beyond belief at the calming effect coloring mandalas has on them. Others have told me they use these coloring books at home or in their offices with a similar effect.

> Delight in the little things.
>
> — *Rudyard Kipling*

My family has "game night" every Saturday night. My ninety-five-year-old mother, my sister and brother-in-law, my cousin Judy, and assorted friends attend. Most of the time, game night follows dinner at Mother's. She still loves to play and experiment with new recipes, and we love to be taste testers for her gourmet meals. Then we play games. The Mexican Train variation of dominoes is our current favorite. We laugh, talk, and share a light-hearted evening.

Give yourself permission to play. Plan a game night. Remember: A crayon reminds us that life isn't a dress rehearsal. Just say "yes" to play and make life a great adventure!

# Activities for Developing Playfulness

1.  **Add playful activities to your life.**

    Below is a list of playful activities. Try one or two of these daily for a month, and notice the change that playing adds to your life.

    - Turn on the radio and dance
    - Read your favorite children's story out loud
    - Take a bubble bath and play in the water
    - Have a water fight
    - Blow up balloons
    - Jump on a trampoline
    - Paint your face or nails a wild color
    - Build a model car or airplane
    - Make mud pies
    - Go to the zoo
    - Buy and read a comic book
    - Bake cookies and eat them with milk
    - Draw a picture and post it on the refrigerator
    - Finger paint
    - Play in the rain
    - Play jacks
    - Hug a tree
    - Giggle
    - Jump rope
    - Color in a coloring book
    - Watch cartoons
    - Swing
    - Build a sand castle
    - Put up a tent and hide inside
    - Skip
    - Blow bubbles

2.  **Take an armchair trip.**

    Decide where you want to travel. Watch movies and read books about the location. Imagine what clothes you'd take. What would you see when you are there? Where would you stay? Set some time aside for this travel fantasy as often as possible. Enjoy your armchair journey.

3.  **Go to a tea room.**

    Wear gloves, a hat, and your best clothes. Remember those days of dress-up and tea parties? Have a tea party and invite your friends.

OR

Have a Super Bowl party any day. Get great food, have a tailgate party, throw a ball around. Have peanuts, popcorn, and Cracker Jacks. Find the prize inside the box and play with it.

4. **Buy a board game.** 

The stores are filled with games for adults. *Scene It* and *Cranium* are two of my favorite games. Puzzles are plentiful, too. Allow yourself to walk the toy aisles of Wal-Mart, K-Mart, and Toys 'R' Us, and read about some of the games. Then buy one and have a game night.

# CHAPTER 17

# A Crayon

## Color Your World

Remember the childhood excitement of opening a new box of crayons? The sight and even the smell of the colored wax filled us with glee! It was hard to decide which one to choose first, since every color looked so wonderful. The crayon reminds us that life needs to be bright and beautiful. We must remember to color our world, our lives, and our days with beauty.

The crayon takes us back to a time when life was simpler. We didn't worry about bills, work, or achievement. We simply added color to paper and played. Let's appreciate the color added to our world through nature. We can take the time to notice the blues in the sky, the reds in the sunrises and sunsets, the greens of the leaves, and the browns of the earth. These simple, colorful, basic beauties surround most of us daily, but we rush through our lives, always on a mission. We forget to notice the delicacy, symmetry, and exquisite coloring of roses, not to mention putting on the brakes for thirty seconds and actually smelling the roses.

Like the orderly color gradation in a box of crayons, our personal environment needs order, too. Things have their proper place. Over the years, I have worked with numerous couples and families who revealed an interesting parallel between the order and beauty in their home and the order and beauty in their relationship. Couples in therapy who complain of serious relationship problems often talk about the mess in their homes, especially in their bedrooms. They describe disarray and visual disaster areas in their homes, areas that are out of control.

> Walk on a rainbow trail; walk on a trail of song, and all about you will be beauty. There is a way out of every dark mist, over a rainbow trail.
>
> — *Edward A. Navajo*

To me it's no wonder their relationships are out of control. How can a healthy relationship exist in chaos, clutter, and darkness? I suggest they go home, move furniture, and de-clutter the home, or at least put the piles into covered baskets. I tell them to throw things out and let go of the old to make room for the "new connections." I suggest lighting dark areas. We need light, color, and order so we can arrange our lives and energize our relationships. Making our homes more beautiful and orderly is not a luxury; it is a necessity. We don't need to spend money to create order and to focus on beauty. Clutter is ugly; simplicity is beautiful. Keep it simple, add color, and maintain order.

While you are adding color to your world, notice the colorful people who are in your life. I remember my Great Aunt Mary. My other great aunts had silver-blue hair. Not Aunt Mary. She had fiery red hair. She dressed in flamboyant, outrageous clothes and smoked cigars! It was the fifties, and nice women wore shirtwaists and pearls. But not my Aunt Mary. She was a character. At parties, she read palms and tea leaves and told wonderful family stories. I remember the excitement I felt when we went to her house or she came to ours. Today we need to embrace colorful people and learn from them.

> No sight that human eyes can look upon is more provocative of awe than is the night sky scattered thick with stars.
>
> — *Llewelyn Powys*

We certainly have colorful people in our society. One need only walk in a shopping mall to see some very colorful people. Pierced eyebrows, noses, and tattoos catch our attention. Hair colors range from basic black to orange, purple, and green, to name a few. Younger generations seem to have given themselves permission to live colorful lives.

The rest of us need to give ourselves permission, as well. Perhaps not in such outrageous ways, but how about adding variety in our friends for a rich, exciting life? Include an array of friends in your life—just like the array of colors in a box of crayons—and they will brighten your days and nights.

The crayon reminds us to create beauty by being interior and exterior "decorators."

# Activities for Coloring Your World

1. **Watch the changing colors of a sunrise or sunset.** ☼

2. **Watch the clouds.** ☁

   On the next warm, sunny day, lie on your back in the grass and watch the clouds roll by. Invite a friend to join you and make up stories of what you see. Draw pictures, too.

3. **Notice the colors of a bird.** ✒

   Are you wearing similar colors?

4. **Associate colors with your feelings.** ✹

   Colors are often associated with feelings and energy:
   - Red—energized, passionate, emotional
   - Blue—sensible, logical
   - Pink—loving, warm, affectionate
   - Green—healing, emotionally balanced, expansive, abundant
   - Orange—communicating well
   - Yellow—open to learning, sunny
   - Purple—spiritual, regal, wise
   - Black—depressed, empty
   - Brown—down to earth
   - Silver—intuitive, clear
   - Gray—confused, cloudy
   - White—clear, open, free

Go through the list. Write down a few of the feelings or energies the colors evoke in you. Does the color of your clothes affect your mood or appearance? Try matching the color you wear to the day's activity.

*Example: Wear orange when you have a special request to communicate to your boss or spouse. A tie or scarf with a little orange will do.*

5. **Create beauty around you.** 

Collect pictures from magazines of rooms you like. Look around your home for an area that needs to be ordered and beautified. Start creating beauty today. Buy a plant or create a backyard or windowsill garden. Find something from the pictures to bring into your room. Move furniture from one room to another.

6. **List the most colorful people in your life.** 

What makes them so bright? Call one of them and make plans for a fun time.

# CHAPTER 18

# A Crayon

## Creativity

A crayon is one of the first tools children use to express creativity, and coloring is one of their favorite pastimes. When we are young, we learn to explore the world of color and beauty with a crayon. Coloring transports us to another place—the playground of the creative mind.

Usually, kids feel more free to be creative than do adults. Coloring was fun and uninhibited until we learned there was a "right way" to color. The person who thought they would help us color "correctly" by telling us to stay inside the lines was actually our first critic. Why can't grass be purple? And who says you have to stay inside the lines?

Often our early childhood experience can leave us marked for life. When my sister Joyce was in kindergarten, she spilled a jar of green paint. The teacher went ballistic and yelled at her. Joyce cried and shook with fear. She never painted again, and to this day thinks she is not creative. However, in the early seventies she

> Imagination is more important than knowledge.
>
> — *Albert Einstein*

graduated college in three years, and began "English as a Second Language" programs in the suburbs of Chicago. She got her master's degree in a year and decided she wanted to speak Spanish more fluently. She went to Barcelona, Spain, with a two-day hotel reservation. She stayed for ten years, starting her own language business. When she returned to the U.S., she decided to try something new. She became a massage therapist and enjoyed a great life in New York City for five years. Then, at forty-six, she decided to move to Florida to be closer to family. She was reading the paper and noticed Continental Airlines was hiring. She had always wanted to be a flight attendant.

> Creativity involves breaking out of established patterns in order to look at things in a different way.
>
> — *Edward DeBono*

So at forty-six, my bilingual sister became a flight attendant, and she wasn't the oldest in the training class! Her flights went to South America, Spain, Puerto Rico, and Santo Domingo.

A few years later, she decided she wanted to learn Italian. She took a month off and lived in Italy and now speaks Italian, too! She spends her time in Rome, Milan, Madrid, Lima, Ecuador, New York City, and even sometimes in Naples, Florida. Yet she thinks that, because she can't paint or draw, she isn't creative.

My sister is a great role model for expressing creativity by living a creative life. Creativity is unleashed in the way we live and view our lives. It is the larger-than-life, thinking-outside-the-box mentality.

In what ways are you creative? Is your work a creative outlet? What about the way you organize your day, your desk, or your home? All of these can be areas of creative expression. Your clothing, cars, possessions, artwork, hobbies, and the way <u>you</u> live your life are creative expressions.

I painted the outside of my house purple. I like purple. It makes me feel serene, peaceful, and creative. Today I drive around town and see at least a dozen purple houses. You never know when you might become a trendsetter!

We can also be creative in our problem-solving techniques. A creative person turns problems into challenges and opportunities. I often use a three-picture drawing technique that I learned from Joyce Mills, psychotherapist, hypnotist and author of *Cartoon Magic*. I ask clients to draw a picture of how the problem looks now; this is picture #1. Picture #2 is how the problem will look when it's "all better." Picture #3 represents what will help the client get from picture #1 to picture #2.

> Every child is an artist. The problem is how to remain an artist once he grows up.
>
> — *Pablo Picasso*

Young children under the age of five are eager to do this artwork. They draw powerful pictures because they both feel and see solutions to their problems. However, most adults whine and fight completing this exercise. They say, "I can't draw," or "I'm not artistic." That early critic controls their ability to try something different and playful.

The three-picture drawing technique activates the entire brain. While you focus on defining the problem, you engage the nonverbal area of the brain through drawing. If you're willing to try, it unlocks a whole new dimension and provides amazing results.

Corporate America has experimented with creative, problem-solving techniques. A few years ago I read an article in *Bottom Line/Personal* magazine that described an innovative technique. When one corporation was faced with a problem, all of its managers sat around a table. Each person was given a different color baseball cap to wear. The green hat was expected to be the creative thinker and generate a lot of ideas. The white hat was the objective thinker and had to concentrate on the facts. The red hat was to express emotions, hunches, and intuitive feelings. The black hat was to be the cautious, negative, doom and gloom, worst-case perspective. The blue hat was to give the objective overview of the entire problem. Something as simple and playful as colored baseball caps generated unorthodox solutions to a complex problem.

Remember to get your crayons out and let your inner child create green cows and pink cats. Rediscover the gift of wonder and look at everything as an amazing adventure. A crayon reminds us that it takes courage to be creative and color outside the lines of life.

# Activities for Developing Creativity

1. **Learn the "Switch Hands Technique."**

   a) Spend two minutes making as long a list as you can of the uses for an ordinary crayon. Now switch to your non-dominant hand and continue the list. You will come up with very different uses for the crayon because this switch activates both sides of the brain.

   b) Write down one of your problems and list some possible solutions. Now switch hands and continue your solution list. This will generate whole-brain problem solving.

2. **Hang out with creative people.**

   If you want to be more creative, you need to spend time with creative people. Contact your local artists' guild and attend meetings or openings. Call some of your most creative friends and go to lunch. Listen to them and notice how they think, dress, and behave. Learn to draw with Betty Edwards' book *Drawing on the Right Side of the Brain*.

3. **Use Joyce Mills' three-picture drawing technique.**

   Think of a problem. Using crayons, draw how the problem looks now. Label that picture #1. Draw how it will look when it's all better, and label that picture #2. Then draw picture #3, which is what is needed to get from picture #1 to picture #2. Post your pictures and experience the change.

4. **When faced with a problem or challenge, try this creative problem-solving technique.** ✎

   Put paper and a crayon next to your bed. Before you go to sleep, try to define the problem, saying it out loud. Then write it down, reviewing all aspects. Repeat the problem before closing your eyes. Three things could happen:
   - Eureka! You will solve the problem in your sleep.
   - You will think of a solution in the next few days.
   - You will not be able to sleep. Two out of three isn't bad.

5. **Think of any problem.** 📖

   Open a book and point to any word. How could you use the word to solve your problem? This helps you to break out of the darkness of the problem and into a more creative light.

6. **Use the "Baseball Cap Technique."** 👪

   If you have a complex problem at home or at work, try the colored baseball cap technique (page 113). Have each friend or family member wear a different color hat, and ask them to stick to their roles. After every person has had a chance to speak freely without being interrupted, watch the group discuss the problem and come up with a solution.

7. **Pretend you are a child.** 🧍 🧍

   Spend fifteen minutes a day, at least once a week, thinking like a child. Walk around your home, neighborhood, or office with the eyes of a five-year-old. Allow yourself to wonder and be amazed.

8. **Add instrumental music as background to any of these activities.** ♫

# A Crayon Reminds Us:

- That it's important to be childlike

- To find beauty around us—to be an interior and exterior decorator

- To color outside the lines

Please use your journal to describe what a crayon symbolizes to you.

# A Candle

# CHAPTER 19

# A Candle

So I just flew in from Florida, and *boy* is my wick tired! But seriously, folks...

## Keep It Light

A candle transforms darkness into light. Of course, to make it happen you must kindle it. A candle is a reminder to light your life with laughter and humor if you want your life to work well.

When I was a high school counselor in the 1970s and 1980s, I had a sign hung on my office door that read: "Humor—never leave home without it." During that time, I finished my degree as an Educational Specialist in Marriage and Family Therapy. My work with families helped me realize that I needed a second sign: "Humor—never *be* home without it."

> When humor goes, there goes civilization.
>
> — *Erma Bombeck*

My father left me many gifts, but two I treasure most are his wit and humor. He always had one silly joke or pun after another. I'm sure glad my last name is "Durante" because I was blessed with two great comedians—my dad and Jimmy Durante—to light my way on the humor path. I'll always remember Jimmy Durante's signature sign-off, "Goodnight, Mrs. Calabash, wherever you are."

Television talk shows and situation comedies reinforce the importance of laughter in our lives. They remind us to keep it light, laugh, and enjoy. Sometimes we laugh at ourselves as we identify with the ridiculous on television. Sometimes, our laughter helps us escape reality for a moment. Whichever, laughter is good medicine. Humor turns something into nothing as we "let it go" and move on. Humor and the ability to laugh have been identified as important ingredients in resilient people. So build your resiliency quotient and laugh a lot.

> Angels can fly because they take themselves lightly.
>
> – *G.K. Chesterton*

Today we are aware of the positive effect humor has on our lives and on our health, both mental and physical. We know that children laugh four hundred times a day, and adults laugh only fifteen times a day. *Laughing Matters* magazine reports that laughing one hundred times a day is the cardiovascular equivalent of ten minutes of rowing. Laughter is good for both the heart and soul, but we also know laughter can be comforting to our bodies.

In the 1970s, research was conducted on hospitalized cancer patients who were receiving heavy doses of morphine every few hours. When these patients were shown *I Love Lucy* reruns at medication time, it was found that their scheduled medications could be delayed by one hour. This is because laughter releases hormones called endorphins, which increase our ability to tolerate pain.

Dr. Patch Adams, the founder and director of The Gesundheit Institute, is known for adding humor to his treatments of patients since 1971. Dr. Adams, a professional clown and performer, as well as a physician, taught the world that combining all the healing arts is essential for wellness. At his center in West Virginia, traditional medicine is integrated with performing arts, arts and crafts, agriculture, recreation, nature, and social services to provide true wellness to his patients. Inspired by Dr. Adams's work, many hospitals have "humor carts" as part of their pain management and wellness programs. The cart holds funny videos, games, and books—all provided to help patients laugh, release endorphins, and shift their focus away from pain.

When my daughter Kirsten was three years old, we had an eye-opening experience. We ran to our van after many hours outside in the cold New Jersey winter. As we entered the van, our heads collided; we hit each other forcefully. She started to cry, and I was blinking back tears. I tried to distract us from our pain.

Since we were blinking, I mentioned that I could wink only my left eye, not my right. Kirsten said she could wink with only her left eye, as well. So, through her tears, she tried to wink her right eye. So did I. We made strange, distorted faces as we struggled to wink. After a few minutes, we were both laughing hysterically. Kirsten looked up through her tears and laughter and said, "You know, Mommy, when you laugh, nothing hurts."

A candle reminds us to brighten our day with lightness and laughter.

So start laughing—or, at the very least, try smiling—and find the humor in daily life. Release those endorphins and have some fun.

# Activities for Keeping It Light

1. **Rent and watch some funny videos.** 👁

   Old classic comedy is wonderful. Look for *The Three Stooges, I Love Lucy*, and *Abbott and Costello*.

2. **Read the comics in the newspaper.** 🔭

   Buy a joke book and read it, or just browse the humor section of the bookstore. Find something that makes you laugh.

3. **Post or frame your favorite cartoon.** 🗄

4. **Smile at people.** ☺

   Do it for the person in the grocery store, or even the person who cuts you off in traffic. Imagine that it is National Smile Day, and just smile all day. Notice how it makes you and others feel.

5. **Make a "Laugh List."** 📄

   Who are the funniest people you know? Make a list with their names and phone numbers. When you need a laugh, call a friend on the list. Thank them for the gift of laughter, humor, and lightness in your life.

6. **Mail your friend something funny.** ✉

   Laughter is contagious. Make someone laugh. Mail your friend a funny comic or joke.

7.  **Attend a humor workshop in Saratoga Springs, N.Y.** ✈

    You will learn a lot and enjoy it, too. To find out more, visit www.humorproject.com.

# CHAPTER 20

# A Candle

## Ritual

A birthday candle heralds another year of life. The birthday ritual is said to have originated in Germany. One candle was placed on the cake for each year, then one extra candle for growth. When the candles were blown out, a wish was made, and the smoke carried the wish to God.

> Rituals are not the path, they are the reminder that there is a path.
>
> — *Emmanuel*

The birthday celebration ritual helps us focus on the future, while reminding us of our connection with the past. The word "ritual" comes from the Latin word *ritus*, or river, which is symbolic of the life force flowing through all living things. Rituals increase balance and connection within ourselves, with others, and with the larger world.

Rituals—repeated ceremonial acts—are integral parts of nature and of our daily lives. They can be conscious or unconscious actions, usually involving some art form, which help to deepen our experience. From birth to death, our lives are shaped by ritualistic behaviors.

You can probably think of many daily habits you do ritualistically, like drinking your morning cup of coffee, reading the newspaper, brushing your teeth, or checking your e-mail or phone messages. These habits become rituals when we consciously think of the action we are performing. We then allow this action to create a sense of safety, security, and order in our day.

> Ceremony and ritual spring from our heart of hearts: those who govern us know it well, for they would sooner deny us bread than dare alter the observance of tradition.
>
> — F. Gonzalez-Crussi

Think of what happens when these rituals are missed. Do you feel "out of it" if you have to rush and miss your morning ritual? Or is rushing part of the morning ritual?

Children are especially comforted by daily rituals. I'm sure you can think of some rituals from your childhood. I remember every night when I went to bed my mother came in and said a bedtime blessing. "May the almighty and merciful God bless you, my child, and keep you safely for time and eternity, for ever and ever, Amen. Goodnight and God bless you." She would then kiss me on the forehead and leave the room. I have continued this tradition with my daughter. For as long as I can remember, I ended her day in a similar way, with the bedtime blessing. Kirsten is now twenty-eight years old and lives in Atlanta, but we talk almost nightly, and I repeat the blessing. If she knows she will be out or busy, she reminds me that she'll say the blessing without me. The ritual has been a form of connection over many years and generations. I'm not really sure if I remember the exact words, but they weren't important. The importance of ritual is in the connection, balance, and security it provides.

One of my favorite books, *The Little Prince* by Antoine de Saint Exupery, reinforces the importance of rituals in relationships. The story is about a little prince from another planet who comes to earth seeking a friend. He meets a fox who teaches him about friendship. They meet daily, but at first the prince comes at nine o'clock, then ten o'clock, etc. The fox tells him to come at the same time because, "You must observe the proper rituals if you want to be tamed. To tame means to establish ties." And how true that is. If we have an established ritual of talking on the phone to our spouse daily at lunch, we worry if the call doesn't come. Or if date night is Friday at eight, you better be on time and ready, or else!

The quick pace of our society leaves ritual gaps where once security lay. The dinner table was often a place of sharing and connection. People sat in the same seats; everyone had specific roles. There was security in this dinnertime routine. With full lives, late nights at work, hockey, baseball, dance, piano lessons, and so on, it has become more and more difficult to make the dinner table sacred. Many families have made breakfast a family ritual. Another idea is to take ten minutes to read together in the morning before the day begins. Whatever you do, find times for daily rituals that connect you to your loved ones.

In addition to daily rituals, ceremonies are often performed at transition times: beginnings (birth and promotions), endings (death), mergers (marriage and partnership), and cycles (birthdays and anniversaries).

Birthday traditions are usually the ones that come to mind when I talk to people. How were your childhood birthdays celebrated? What special traditions or foods did you have? I remember birthdays were a very special time in my family. There were always two parties—one for the birthday child and his/her friends, and one for all the adults and family. Food was plentiful, from pasta to pastry. But the cake was the main event of the party! For many years it was a doll cake—a lovely doll with a cake dress. After her dress was consumed by wide-eyed friends, she became my doll to dress up and play with for the year. On my fiftieth birthday, my mother made me a doll cake—her own version—but it was a wonderful reminder of those great celebrations.

As our society has grown and aged, we have failed to keep our rituals current with society's needs. Although we badly need rituals, we have many transition times that lack them. American society is in need of a transition ritual from adolescence to adulthood—a rite of

passage. We are one of the few cultures lacking this ritual, and we are faced with serious problems because of it. Teenagers create their own rituals for self-discovery, social connection, and tradition. They may pierce and tattoo body parts or assume their own style of dress. Gangs form because kids want to feel they are a part of something, even if it's destructive.

Without a ceremony, or some form of encouragement to move away from destructive behaviors, people can get stuck in adolescence and wreak havoc on society. In some ancient civilizations, a boy went into the woods to be initiated into manhood by his elders. Ceremonies were held for girls when they started menstruation to acknowledge their passage into womanhood.

Adults lack rituals, too. We need to acknowledge transition times, such as retirement and divorce. Rituals help us realize that generations before us have had the same experience, that we are not isolated, and that other people's experience can help guide us through the transition.

I encourage you to look at your life and identify places where rituals could be helpful. One simple, comforting ritual I enjoy is the "Red Plate Ritual." This ritual is said to have been started by early American settlers. Written on the plate are the words, "Today you are special." The plate may be used to honor a birthday, promotion, or good grades. Maybe you had a hard day. Take out the plate, and it will lift your spirits. I also use the plate at buffet dinner parties. Someone ends up with it and feels very special. If you don't have a red plate, make one at your local ceramic hut. How about red paper plates with the message written with a gold marker? The Red Plate Ritual affords us time to focus on and share the event with others.

The candle symbolizes the value of ceremonial acts. It reminds us to stop, think, and appreciate a ritual. Be conscious of your habits and transform them into rituals. Go ahead and add some meaningful rituals to your life.

# Activities for Enhancing Your Life Through Rituals

1. **List three of your rituals.** 🖊

   Think of three daily rituals that you do almost unconsciously. Make them conscious. Be aware of their importance in your day. Appreciate the ritual for the comfort it adds to your life.

2. **Add a new beginning ritual to your day.** 💬

   For example, you could read an inspirational quote to start your morning in a positive, focused way.

3. **Examine your closing rituals for the day.** 🗨

   Do you have a bedtime ritual? Children need bedtime rituals, and so do adults. You could say a prayer of thanks for what you received that day: nourishing food, good health, love, the beauty of nature, etc.

4. **Create rituals where they are lacking.** 🏆

   If you earn a promotion, honor your achievement with a celebration. Give an award to a parent for outstanding love and guidance. Our society doesn't have a ritual for divorce other than the issuing of a certificate. It's no wonder that many couples have trouble with closure. Perhaps we could have a few close friends and family members witness a ceremony that acknowledges the dissolution of the marriage. Depending on the situation, you could even have a divorce party to celebrate the start of a new chapter in your life.

5. **Review holiday rituals.** ☑

Decide what fits and what needs to be altered. Are your rituals rich with meaning or only the hollow vestiges of ceremonies?

# CHAPTER 21

# A Candle
## Aging Gracefully

W hen we were children we couldn't wait for our birthday celebrations. But somewhere along the way we began to dread birthdays because they reminded us that we were getting older.

The candle reminds us that aging is inevitable, but that doesn't make it bad. In a society that worships youth, it's difficult to realize that we gain value and get better with age. Somehow we must educate society about the positive aspects of aging. Our appearance changes with age, but that doesn't mean it's less beautiful. Just as we can appreciate a fine, aged wine, we need to learn to honor our vintage bodies and Solomonic wisdom.

> The greatest thing about getting old is that you don't lose all the other ages you've been.
>
> — *Madeleine L'Engle*

Many studies have focused on aging and the ingredients for aging well. Oprah said "Fifty is the new thirty," so I guess that sixty is the new forty—sounds good to me! The American Medical Association stresses being active as a core factor to healthy aging. We know healthy eating plays another important role. My favorite study, however, is "The Nun Study." A group of Catholic nuns in Minnesota were studied as they aged. All lived well into their eighties and nineties, with relatively good physical health; but more importantly, they were mentally intact. The nuns continued to work well into their seventies. They lived in a community and shared friendships rich with laughter and spirituality.

When I lecture, I ask my audiences to suggest other reasons for the nuns' long and healthy lives. Most reply that it was because they had no husbands or children, but "The Nun Study" did not come to the same conclusion. While it is true that family life can add stress to one's life, it also adds much joy.

> Be not afraid of
> growing slowly,
> be afraid only of
> standing still.
>
> — *Chinese Proverb*

The study did reveal another interesting fact. When the young women joined the convent, they were asked to write the story of their life before becoming a nun. The stories that contained detailed and positive memories equated to a longer, "brain-healthy" life for the nun. I guess we all need to get our pencils and begin writing!

The candle is a symbol for celebrating and honoring each passing year. The challenge is to validate and glorify *every* age by creating new realities. For example, how can we make our forties carefree, fun, and exciting—reminiscent of those childhood days? How do we incorporate into our sixties the risk-taking, adventuresome spirit and dare-to-be-different attitude of adolescence?

When the first group of Baby Boomers reached sixty—and the rest were fast approaching the second half of life—they demanded that the old beliefs of aging be debunked. It used to be an anomaly to see people in their late fifties starting a new business, climbing Mt. Fuji, or finishing their college degree. Now we all know many such active, inspired people.

> Old age ain't for sissies.
>
> —Bette Davis

"Grow old along with me; the best is yet to be" is a wonderful motto for aging gracefully. This Robert Browning quote reminds us to both find and become role models for all of life's cycles, and to actually look forward to aging. Let's choose to make peace with our past, our bodies, and ourselves so we can focus on the best that is yet to be.

Older people exude a certain wisdom that is attained by decades of experience. When I look in the mirror at sixty, I wonder about this face that looks back at me—the wrinkles, the drooping cheeks, the thinning lips and disappearing chin. But the eyes are still the same. They smile back at me with a twinkle, and I realize I am more than my body. I have lived long, engaged in many relationships, and weathered many emotional ups and downs. I have discerned who I am and what I want. I have learned about the world and the nature of reality. I have come to understand and appreciate solitude and the power of silence and reflection. I have learned to not be afraid to act on my

> We grow neither better nor worse as we get old, but more like ourselves.
>
> — May Lamberton Becker

hunches. I know I create life as I go. I worry less about what others think and more about what I think. I am more comfortable and grounded in being okay with ME! I wish the same for you.

Perhaps we can learn from Asian and Native American cultures to value the wisdom of elders. These cultures know that to age gracefully, we must incorporate solitude into our lives. Let's give ourselves the gift of silence by creating a quiet space, by taking the time to reflect, to meditate, and to connect with nature and with our God.

The candle reminds us that we can walk or run gracefully into the cycles of aging. May you enjoy your journey.

# Activities for Aging Gracefully

1. **Talk to a senior.**

   Interview someone who is at least five or ten years your senior. Ask them about their life in recent years. What have they learned and experienced about themselves and their bodies? Ask them to focus on the positive.

2. **Title your life.**

   Write a title for each decade of your life using a song, book, or movie title.

   *Example:*
   - *The twenties,* Love Story
   - *The thirties,* A League of Her Own
   - *The forties,* How Dianne Got Her Groove Back

   *Write some titles for future decades like* Fabulously Freeing Fifties, Sixties Serene and Secure at Last.

3. **Write a life script.**

   Use the scripting technique (refer to the Chapter 13 Activities for Enlivening Written Communication, pages 84 and 85), and create a script for the way you'd like your next few decades to look.

4. **Find role models.**

   Choose people whom you admire—those who are aging gracefully. These could be famous people, like actress Katherine Hepburn, or people you know.

a) Post pictures of them. Use them as role models. I have a picture of actress Sophia Loren on my refrigerator.

b) Spend time with these role models or mentors, if possible. Listen to their stories, and share memories and dreams.

5. **Connect in your community.** ☙

Have coffee and chat with an elderly neighbor or someone in a retirement community or nursing home.

# A Candle Reminds Us:

- That when you laugh, nothing hurts

- To value ceremonial acts

- To grow old gracefully (and gratefully)

Describe in your journal what a candle symbolizes to you.

# A Seashell

# CHAPTER 22

# A Seashell

## Protection

When I first began giving my "Happiness: It's in the Bag!™" lecture, one of the symbols was a seashell, something very plentiful here in Naples, Florida. Seashells can be found in almost every home, and I keep a large basket of them in my counseling office.

When clients have experienced a particularly difficult or painful session, I present them with a seashell. I remind them that, at certain times, we have to be more careful and protect ourselves. I tell them the story of hermit crabs, which live on the ocean floor. These crabs have a hard skin, except for the abdomen, which is soft. To protect their soft spot, they find a shell and make it their home. The shell is never a perfect fit and, as they grow, they need to shed their old shell and find a new one. When a hermit crab is threatened, it withdraws into its shell until the danger has passed.

> When you come to a roadblock, take a detour.
>
> — Mary Kay Ash

The hermit crab's journey is symbolic of our life journeys. We live in a world that can be frightening, as well as exciting. During times of transition—when our relationships end, our health suffers, we lose a job or have a crisis in our family—our hard skin may not be hard enough. We feel that our soft belly is exposed, making us vulnerable, so we seek a shell for safety. When it's safe, we come out and try again. We may go through this process many times in our life. In fact, every day is a new journey in the open sea of life.

> Every now and then, have a little relaxation. For when you come back to your work, your judgment will be surer.
>
> — *Leonardo DaVinci*

We live in a sleep-deprived society. We are on a fast track that is going ever faster, and sleep is seen by some as a waste of time—even frivolous, perhaps. Sleep studies indicate that eight hours of sleep for adults is important to maintaining maximum health. In the health section of the May 2006 issue of *Positive Thinking Magazine*, Michael F. Roizen, M.D., and Mehmet C. Oz, M.D., compare massive sleep deprivation to a "tequila bender." Additionally, they cite a study where doctors who work eighty to ninety hours per week performed in a simulated driving test as though they had "chugged three to four alcoholic beverages."

In yet another study, involving nurses who worked 12.5 hours or more on their shifts, the researchers found that these nurses were "three times more likely to make mistakes than nurses who worked shorter shifts."

Other sleep studies point to the fact that people are happier, work more efficiently, and sleep better when they give their bodies the needed time to recuperate and renew themselves through sleep. Sleep is even more important when we are going through stressful times.

Thomas Edison was aware of the importance of sleep, and he seemed to take the idea of sleep to a new level. A story is told about how Mrs. Edison always worried because Tom never wanted to stop creating and go to bed. She had a cot put inside his laboratory. Edison, knowing the importance of sleep, was renowned for taking "catnaps." He was able to put himself into a relaxed, trance-like state and wake with new solutions to the problems with his creations. "When you get quiet, it just dawns on you," was Edison's mantra when he referred to his catnaps.

It certainly worked for him. History has demonstrated the quantity and quality of his extremely important inventions, which have benefited us all. Many corporations today have created "nap rooms" for their employees—perhaps in the hopes of creating more Edison-like thinking and problem-solving possibilities for their employees.

I am blessed with a very busy private counseling practice and an office with two large sofas. Many days, I stretch out, close my eyes, and get quiet. I awaken five minutes later, refreshed and ready to listen more attentively to my next client.

Catnaps, a good night's sleep, and resting are all important ways we care for and protect our body and our mind. A seashell serves as a reminder to slow down, protect yourself, and rest.

# Activities for Creating Protection

1. **List five healthy ways you protected yourself when you were the most vulnerable.** 📄

   Be aware that it's okay to have vulnerable times and to hide out for a while until you get stronger. It's also okay to keep yourself out of harm's way. For example, if you have an alcohol addiction, don't hang out at the bar.

2. **Observe the ways you rest this week.**

   Rest includes not only sleeping, but napping, meditating, and reclining. Make adjustments if you frequently feel fatigued.

3. **Think of three times that you had to let go of an old shell.** 🦪

   Perhaps you had to let go through a move, divorce, death, or marriage. Rate how vulnerable you felt on a scale of one to five—five being the most vulnerable. What new shell did you find to replace the old?

# CHAPTER 23

# A Seashell

## One of a Kind

When I walk on the beach, I am struck by the diversity and uniqueness of the shells. Seashells come in so many sizes, shapes, and colors. There are billions of them on the beach, but no two are exactly alike. Often it's the small shells that catch our attention, and we can spend hours collecting them. At other times, we may opt only for one large conch with a shiny, pink interior. It sometimes seems easier to see uniqueness in seashells than in ourselves.

Our high-tech society thrives on mass production, which can make uniqueness and diversity difficult qualities to maintain. We want to have what others have; yet we want it to be uniquely our own, like a designer shirt in a rare color. Paradoxically, we want to belong; yet we want to be different. We are constantly striving for the balance between these two—belonging and uniqueness—both vital ingredients for healthy self-esteem.

When we look at the beach from a distance, we see an exquisite

> Two roads
> diverged in a
> wood, and I—I
> took the one less
> traveled by, and
> that has made all
> the difference.
>
> — *Robert Frost*

expanse of sand and shells. On closer inspection, we see that, while some shells are perfect, many are broken, chipped, or worn down; however, they all contribute to making a beautiful beach.

The following story illustrates how no one is perfect, but people love us, regardless:

A water bearer in India carried two large pots on the end of a pole. He went daily to the stream and returned to his master's house with water. One of the pots was perfect, while the other had a crack, leaking at least half of its contents before the servant reached his master's home. After a year, the perfect pot was proud of its accomplishment. However, the cracked pot was ashamed of its flaw and apologized for its inability to provide a full pot of water at the end of each day's journey.

The water bearer told the cracked pot to notice the road as they returned from the stream. The cracked pot watched and saw a wide variety of beautiful flowers blooming only on one side of the road.

The water bearer said, "I have always known about your flaw, so I took advantage of it. I planted flower seeds on your side of the road. Every day you watered them. If you hadn't been just the way you are, I wouldn't have been able to pick those beautiful flowers to grace my master's table."

Each of us has our own strengths and flaws, just like the pots in the story or the seashells on the beach. Uniqueness is what sets us apart from the others. Our gift might be that we can make others laugh or that we live our life with integrity. The seashell reminds us that each of us is one of a kind and can celebrate our unique qualities.

# Activities for Celebrating Your Unique Qualities

1. **Where do you shine?** 📄

   Make a list of your special talents or gifts and post it on the mirror. How are you using them in your life?

2. **Be thankful.** 🎁

   Every day for the next week, give thanks for your gifts and talents.

3. **Write a thank-you note to yourself.** ✏️

   Thank yourself for who you are and what you do that is special.

4. **Examine your wardrobe, home, or office.** 🏠

   Do you have a unique style? Do you have certain collections, a special flair, or a special color that dominates?

5. **Determine what else you would like to do.** **?**

   If you had three other lives to live, who would you be? Are you incorporating any of those talents into your life now? Could you?

6. **Create a personal uniqueness alphabet.** abc

   *For example:*

   *A—Artistic*

   *B—Balanced*

   *C—Creative*

7. **Draw a picture of your uniqueness.** 🖋

# CHAPTER 24

# A Seashell
## Mother Nature

The seashell reminds us that we live in an interconnected web of life. We are not isolated from nature or from one another. Throw a shell or pebble into a pond and watch how the whole pond is affected by the ripples from one small object. In our consumer-driven, information-based culture, we often forget the importance of our relationship to the natural environment.

Ancient cultures revered Mother Nature. They observed her power, not only in the sea, but in the earth, the air, and fire, as well. Most of the indigenous peoples of the earth continue to respect nature, and walking in harmony with the earth is an integral part of their teachings. There is much we could learn from Native Americans and other cultures about being stewards of the earth.

Modern scientists are still infants in their ability to know and control Mother Nature. We have become intensely aware of our powerlessness as we experience one natural challenge after another. Tsunamis in Indonesia killed hundreds of thousands. Major hurricanes in the southeast devastated American cities. Earthquakes in India and

Japan annihilated villages. Tornadoes, forest fires, and floods spread through areas of the world leaving chaos and millions of lives changed forever. Time and again, we stand in awe of our impotence and insignificance in relation to nature's majestic power.

> This we know—the earth does not belong to man—man belongs to the earth ...
> Whatever befalls the earth befalls the sons of the earth. Man did not weave the web of life. He is merely a strand of it. Whatever he does to the web, he does to himself.
>
> — *Chief Seattle*

Yet man has long known the benefits of nature's gifts. Sunshine helps plants and humans thrive. Scientists have proven that ultraviolet frequencies can induce a feeling of general well-being because they rewire our biological and hormonal systems. We feel better in light and sunshine. Full spectrum light bulbs were developed to mirror the effects of the sun inside the home. The population growth in the sunshine states seems to reinforce this concept.

Plants, one of nature's gifts, have been used for thousands of years to heal both the body and mind. Ginkgo is the 270 million-year-old version of Prozac. Many studies in Scandinavian countries show Ginkgo effectively treats seasonal affective disorder. Seasonal affective disorder, or SAD, is a form of depression that can affect people during darker fall and winter months.

Another gift from Mother Nature is one of my favorites—aromatherapy. Biologists and researchers in the field of olfactory science agree that certain scents, when inhaled, lead to improved mental status, relieve stress, and ease the pain of change and difficult transitions. As a therapist working with anxious and depressed clients, I leapt for joy when I met Candace Newman, an aromatherapist known as "the oil lady." She introduced me to aromas and their healing powers.

One of my clients, Mary, a sixty-five-year-old Midwesterner, had suffered from many health crises. She had been in a coma for four months following bypass surgery. As she was healing, she had a setback when she fell and broke her leg. She became very anxious about leaving the house. Since she had terrible reactions to prescription medications, I sent her to Candace. Mary was invited to smell a variety of essential oils—orange, lavender, rose, and peppermint. Candace selected lavender for Mary to use as a natural tranquilizer. Now, a year later, Mary still carries the lavender in her purse or pocket. At the first sign of anxiety, she takes a long, inhaling breath, which calms her instantly. Mary has become a firm believer in aromatherapy. She feels it has saved her life—a beautiful gift from Mother Nature and Candace.

I keep small bottles of essential oils in my office and often have clients smell them to find relief from their present problems. The results are truly amazing. I also start my day by using a rose lavender spray to keep me calm and centered.

The next time you're having a bad day, take a walk in nature and touch the earth. Notice the surroundings. As you connect with nature, you will feel better. Being in nature helps us to get out of the swirling problems in our minds and back into the enjoyment of simple, sensory pleasures—back to living and enjoying the present moment.

I wrote much of this book at the beach while listening to the call of the seagulls and the lapping of the waves against the shore. My thinking expands with the warmth of the sun. While you may not have the opportunity to sit at the beach, you can still leave your everyday world of concrete and mortar to spend some time in nature. Even in Manhattan you can visit Central Park and experience the wind blowing through the trees or feel the mist coming off a pond.

Without the gifts of the earth, we cannot survive. By appreciating and preserving these gifts, we and our offspring will thrive for generations to come. A seashell reminds us to nourish our relationship with Mother Nature and celebrate Earth Day every day.

# Activities for Connecting to Mother Nature

1. **Take a nature walk.**

   Be present and experience your surroundings. Finetune your senses. Feel the wind, breathe in the smells, hear the sounds, and see the colors.

2. **Touch the earth today.**

   Collect some small items from nature—a leaf, a shell, driftwood, or a flower. Keep them nearby as reminders of your connection with the earth.

3. **Acknowledge Mother Nature.**

   Start the day off with a silent salute to Mother Nature, which has a way of bringing solace to all troubles.

4. **Do two or three deeds this week for the earth.**

   Pick up litter, donate your time or money to an environmental organization, recycle, or plant a tree.

5. **Collect wildlife or nature art.**

   Go to art shows or museums. Albinarts.com is a wonderful website with great nature photography.

6. **Read about essential oils.** 📚

Try them. Smell lavender, orange, and rose. Visit Candace Newman's website at www.goodmedicinetin.com.

# A Seashell Reminds Us:

- To protect and rest our body and our mind

- To celebrate our unique qualities

- That we should nourish our connection with the earth

Describe in your journal what a seashell symbolizes to you.

# Your Everyday Symbols

# Epilogue

*Everyday Symbols for Joyful Living* can start you on an adventure in creative symbolism. The book's light and simple format is meant to help clarify your life's priorities and values.

To make this a more personal connection, it's time for you to look at your life and see if there are any missing ingredients. If so, what other symbol could you cook up for the quality you need to enhance?

A few suggestions:
- A feather for lightness or quietness
- A rose for more beauty or delicacy
- A paper clip to hold it all together
- A band-aid to cover and heal the wounds
- A pair of ruby slippers to help you return home

It's up to you. Go wild!

> *Life is full of symbols to help me see*
> *How to learn, to grow, and just be me.*
> *When I forget to look within*
> *And all my feelings are in a spin,*
> *This book of symbols takes me where*
> *I learn to handle me with care.*

# BiblioTherapy

Albom, Mitch. *Tuesdays with Morrie: An Old Man, a Young Man, and Life's Greatest Lesson.* New York, NY, Doubleday, 1997.

Bartfeld, Martha. *Magic Mandala Coloring Book.* Santa Fe, NM, Mandalart Creations, 1998.

Beattie, Melody. *The Language of Letting Go.* Center City, MN, Hazelden, 1996.

Beck, Renee, and Metrick, Sydney Barbara. *The Art of Ritual: Creating and Performing Ceremonies for Growth and Change.* Berkley, CA, Celestial Arts, 2003.

Bombeck, Erma. *All I Know about Animal Behavior I Learned in Loehman's Dressing Room.* New York, NY, HarperCollins, 1995.

Bombeck, Erma. *Family – The Ties that Bind...and Gag!* New York, NY, Fawcett Books, 1988.

Bombeck, Erma. *Motherhood: The Second Oldest Profession.* New York, NY, Dell, 1987.

Borysenko, Joan, and Dveirin, Gordon F. *Saying Yes to Change.* Carlsbad, CA, Hay House, 2006.

Braiker, Harriet, Ph.D. *The Disease to Please.* New York, NY, McGraw-Hill, 2001.

Breathnach, Sarah Ban. *Moving On: Creating Your House of Belonging with Simple Abundance.* Des Moines, IA, Meredith Books, 2006.

Breathnach, Sarah Ban. *Simple Abundance: A Daybook of Comfort and Joy.* New York, NY, Warner Books, 1995.

Buscaglia, Leo F. *Living, Loving, and Learning.* New York, NY, Ballantine Books, 1982.

Cameron, Julia. *The Artist's Way: A Spiritual Path to Higher Creativity.* New York, NY, Penguin Putnam, 1992.

Canfield, Jack, and Hansen, Mark Victor. *Chicken Soup for the Soul.* Deerfield Beach, FL, HCI, 1995.

Carle, Eric. *A House for Hermit Crab.* Riverside, NJ, Simon and Schuster, 2002.

Carlson, Richard. *Don't Sweat the Small Stuff.* New York, NY, Hyperion, 1997.

Carlson, Richard. *What about the Big Stuff?* New York, NY, Hyperion, 2002.

Costanzo, Charlene. *The Twelve Gifts in Marriage.* New York, NY, HarperCollins, 2005.

Costanzo, Charlene. *The Twelve Gifts of Birth.* New York, NY, HarperCollins, 1999.

Crowley, Richard J., and Mills, Joyce C. *Cartoon Magic: How to Help Children Discover Their Rainbows Within.* Washington, DC, Magination Press, 1989.

De Saint-Exupery, Antoine. *The Little Prince.* Orlando, FL, Harcourt, Inc., 1943.

Doherty, Dorothy Albrecht, and McNamara, Mary Colgan. *Out of the Skin into the Soul: The Art of Aging.* Philadelphia, PA, Innisfree Press, 1993.

Edwards, Betty. *Drawing on the Right Side of the Brain.* New York, NY, Tarcher, 1989.

Ford, Linda, and Goodman, Beth. *The Owner's Manual: A Fast, Fun, and Easy Way to Knowing and Understanding Your Lover.* La Jolla, CA, The Ford Group, 1993.

Frankl, Viktor E. *Man's Search for Meaning.* New York, NY, Pocket Books, 1997.

Fulghum, Robert. *From Beginning to End: The Rituals of Our Lives.* New York, NY,

Villard Books, 1995.

Gafni, Marc. *Soul Prints: Your Path to Fulfillment.* New York, NY, Fireside, 2002.

Hay, Louise. *Meditations to Heal Your Life.* Carlsbad, CA, Hay House, 2002.

Hay, Louise. *You Can Heal Your Life.* Carlsbad, CA, Hay House, 1999.

Hope, Bob, and Hope, Linda. *Bob Hope: My Life in Jokes.* New York, NY, Hyperion, 2003.

Imber-Black, Evan, Ph.D., and Roberts, Janine, Ed.D. *Rituals for Our Times: Celebrating, Healing, and Changing our Lives and Our Relationships.* Lanham, MD, Jason Aronson Books, 1998.

Jeffers, Susan. *Feel the Fear and Do It Anyway.* New York, NY, Ballantine Books, 1988.

Jones, Laurie Beth. *The Path: Creating Your Mission Statement for Work and for Life.* New York, NY, Hyperion, 1998.

Keating, Kathleen. *The Hug Therapy Book.* Minneapolis, MN, CompCare Publishers, 1983.

Lerner, Harriet. *The Dance of Anger: A Woman's Guide to Changing the Patterns of Intimate Relationships.* New York, NY, HarperCollins, 1985.

Lerner, Harriet. *The Dance of Intimacy: A Woman's Guide to Courageous Acts of Change in Key Relationships.* New York, NY, Harper & Row, 1990.

Lindburgh, Anne Morrow. *Gift from the Sea.* New York, NY, Pantheon Books, 1991.

Lobenstine, Margaret. *The Renaissance Soul: Life Design for People with Too Many Passions to Pick Just One.* New York, NY, Broadway Books, 2006.

Louden, Jennifer. *The Couples' Comfort Book: A Creative Guide to Renewing Passion, Pleasure, and Commitment.* New York, NY, HarperCollins, 1994.

Louden, Jennifer. *The Woman's Comfort Book: A Self-Nurturing Guide for Restoring*

*Balance in Your Life.* New York, NY, HarperCollins, 1992.

Lysne, Robin Heerens. *Dancing Up the Moon: A Woman's Guide to Creating Traditions that Bring Sacredness to Daily Life.* Emeryville, CA, Conari Press, 1995.

McKay, Matthew, and Rogers, Peter. *The Anger Control Workbook.* Oakland, CA, New Harbinger Publications, 2000.

McWilliams, Peter, Bloomfield, Harold, and Colgrove, Melba. *How to Survive the Loss of a Love.* Los Angeles, CA, Prelude Press, 1993.

Millman, Dan. *The Laws of Spirit: A Tale of Transformation.* Tiburon, CA, HJ Kramer, 1995.

Millman, Dan. *The Life You Were Born to Live: A Guide to Finding Your Life Purpose.* Tiburon, CA, HJ Kramer, 1995.

Millman, Dan. *Way of the Peaceful Warrior, 20th Anniversary Edition: A Book that Changes Lives.* Tiburon, CA, HJ Kramer, 2000.

Myss, Caroline. *Anatomy of the Spirit: The Seven Stages of Power and Healing.* New York, NY, Three Rivers Press, 1996.

Myss, Caroline. *Sacred Contracts: Awakening Your Divine Potential.* New York, NY, Three Rivers Press, 2003.

Orman, Suze. *The Courage to be Rich: Creating a Life of Material and Spiritual Abundance.* New York, NY, Riverhead Books, 1999.

Pearsall, Paul, Ph.D. *The Beethoven Factor: The New Positive Psychology of Hardiness, Happiness, Healing, and Hope.* Charlottesville, VA, Hampton Roads Publishing Co., 2003.

Pearsall, Paul, Ph.D. *The Heart's Code.* New York, NY, Broadway Books, 1999.

Pearsall, Paul, Ph.D. *Toxic Success: How to Stop Striving and Start Thriving.* Makawao, Maui, HI, Inner Ocean Publishing, Inc., 2002.

Quindlen, Anna. *A Short Guide to a Happy Life.* New York, NY, Random House, 2000.

Rogers, Fred. *The World According to Mr. Rogers.* New York, NY, Hyperion, 2003.

Ruiz, Don Miguel. *The Four Agreements: A Practical Guide to Personal Freedom.* San Rafael, CA, Amber-Allen Publishing, 1997.

SARK. *Prosperity Pie: How to Relax about Money and Everything Else.* New York, NY, Fireside, 2002.

SARK. *Succulent Wild Women.* New York, NY, Fireside, 1997.

SARK. *Transformation Soup: Healing for the Splendidly Imperfect.* New York, NY, Fireside, 2000.

Sher, Barbara, and Gottlieb, Annie. *Wishcraft: How to Get What You Really Want.* New York, NY, Ballantine Books, 2003.

Simon, Dr. Sidney B., and Simon, Suzanne. *Forgiveness: How to Make Peace with Your Past and Get on with Your Life.* New York, NY, Warner Books, 1991.

Smith, Keri. *Living Out Loud: Activities to Fuel a Creative Life.* San Francisco, CA, Chronicle Books, LLC, 2003.

Stock, Gregory. *The Book of Questions.* New York, NY, Workman Publishing, 1987.

Von Oech, Roger. *Creative Whack Pack.* Stamford, CT, U.S. Games Systems, 1989.

Williamson, Marianne. *The Gift of Change: Spiritual Guidance for a Radically New Life.* New York, NY, HarperCollins, 2004.

Wiseman, Richard. *The Luck Factor: The Four Essential Principles.* New York, NY, Hyperion, 2003.

Wolin, Steven J., M.D., and Wolin, Sybil, Ph.D. *The Resilient Self: How Survivors of Troubled Families Rise Above Adversity.* New York, NY, Villard Books, 1993.

# Websites

www.albinarts.com

www.bottomlinesecrets.com

www.ciweb.org

www.eomega.org

www.goodmedicinetin.com

www.humorproject.com

www.kerismith.com

www.makethedashcount.com

www.marthabartfeld.com

www.naturalawakeningsmag.com

www.patchadams.org

www.positivethinkingmag.com

www.spiritualityhealth.com

www.templetonpress.com

www.thetwelvegifts.com

# Index

## A

abandonment, 42 (see also alone, isolation, and loneliness)
abuse, 41, 43, 87
achievement, 95, 105, 131
acknowledgment, 62, 68, 130, 131, 155
"acting out," 42
Activities
  for Aging Gracefully, 137, 138
  for Arousing Passion, 50
  for Celebrating Your Unique Qualities, 148
  for Coloring Your World, 108, 109
  for Connecting to Mother Nature, 155, 156
  for Creating Caring Contact and Connection, 45
  for Creating Protection, 145
  for Developing an "I Can" Attitude, 20, 21
  for Developing Creativity, 114–116
  for Developing Playfulness, 103, 104
  for Developing Resiliency, 70, 71
  for Developing Appropriate Risk-Taking, 64, 65
  for Developing Spiritual Insight, 31, 32
  for Enhancing Communication, 9, 10
  for Enhancing Your Life Through Rituals, 131, 132
  for Enlivening Written Communication, 84, 85
  for Erasing Mistakes and Moving on, 94, 95
  for Experiencing the Pleasures of Chocolate, 39
  for Keeping It Light, 124, 125
  for Releasing Emotions, 89, 90
  for Seeing Different Sides, 13–15
  for Stretching the Body, 75
  for Understanding Your Money Dynamics, 26, 27
  for Unwrapping the Foil, 55
Adams, Dr. Patch, 122
addiction, 36, 37, 145 (see also alcohol)
adolescence, 129, 134 (see also teenagers)
adventure, 55, 102, 113, 134, 160
adversaries, 11
adversity, 7, 165
aggravation, 88
aggressiveness, 90
aging, 133–138
alcohol, 69, 143, 145 (see also addiction)
alienation, 90
alone, 13, 54, 55, 68, 69 (see also abandonment, isolation, and loneliness)
AMA Research Study, 43
American Medical Association (AMA), 43, 133
anger, 18, 42, 86–89, 92–94, 163, 164 (see also rage and unresolved anger)
animals, 29, 41, 45, 161 (see also dogs and pets)
anniversaries, 128
antioxidants, 37
anxiety, 29, 61, 75, 90, 152, 153 (see also stress)
apologies, 89, 91–95, 147 (see also sorry)

armchairs, 103
arms crossed, 9
aromatherapy, 152, 153
art, 6, 28, 29, 101, 112, 114, 122, 127, 149,
    155, 161, 162, 166
artists, 84, 101, 112, 114, 149, 162
*Artist's Way, The*, 84, 162
Ash, Mary Kay, 142
attention, 7, 10, 12, 21, 22, 25, 33, 107,
    146
attitude, 16, 17, 20, 67, 134
Aurelius, Marcus, 88
"Autobiography in Five Short Chapters,"
    66, 67
awards, 131
awareness, 15, 27, 46, 60, 88, 121, 131,
    144, 145, 151

# B

Baby Boomers, 134
balance, 3, 18, 23, 24, 61, 108, 126, 128,
    146, 149, 164
Bartfeld, Martha, 102, 161, 166
"Baseball Cap Technique," 113, 115
beauty, 17, 28, 53, 102, 105–107, 109, 110,
    117, 131, 133, 147, 153, 160
Becker, May Lamberton, 135
bedroom, the, 49, 106 (see also "fine
    dining" sex, libido, "make love,"
    physical love, quickies, and sex)
bedtime rituals, 131
behavior, 10, 12, 42, 89, 127, 129, 161
    inappropriate, 42, 86
    violent, 42, 43
beliefs, 28, 29, 31, 32, 68, 135 (see also
    faith, God, higher power,
    prayer, and religion)
belonging, 146
biologists, 152
birth order, 100
Blake, William, 93
blood flow, 37, 84
blood pressure, 29, 37, 41, 86

body language, 9 (see also facial
    expressions and nonverbal
    communication)
Bombeck, Erma, 120, 161
books, 3, 16, 32, 37, 47, 49, 54, 68, 85,
    100, 102, 103, 114, 115, 122,
    124, 128, 137, 153, 160–165 (see
    also literature)
both sides, 11, 12, 33, 114
*Bottom Line/Personal* magazine, 113
bouncing back, 66, 69, 70 (see also
    resiliency and snapping back)
brain, 1, 73, 81, 112, 114, 134, 162
    alpha and theta waves of, 29
    research of the, 1
"brain drain," 84
brainstorm, 11, 14
breathing, 13, 39, 43, 73–76, 81, 95, 100,
    153, 155 (see also deep breaths)
Browning, Robert, 135
Buck, Pearl S., 62
Buscaglia, Dr. Leo (Dr. Hug), 43, 60, 162

# C

calmness, 75, 102, 153
Cameron, Julia, 84
candle, 2, 49, 119, 120, 122, 126, 130, 133,
    134, 136, 139
cardiovascular system, 43, 121
caresses, 40, 41
caring contact, 40, 45, 56
Carter, former President Jimmy, 47
*Cartoon Magic*, 112, 162
"catnaps," 144 (see also naps, rest, and
    sleep)
conflict, 13, 22, 32, 40, 88, 90, 92
celebrations, 38, 126, 129, 131–133, 148,
    154, 157
censoring, 14, 22, 86, 89
ceremonies, 127–132, 161
challenges, 63, 66, 112, 115, 134, 151
change, 12, 17, 20, 22, 28, 31, 48, 49, 53,
    55, 60–64, 66, 68, 85, 94, 95,

103, 114, 133, 152, 161, 163–
165 (see also transition)
Chesterton, G.K., 121
childhood, 20, 69, 100, 105, 110, 127,
129, 134
children, 20, 26, 40–42, 45, 47, 48, 50,
55, 81, 82, 87, 100, 102, 103,
110, 112, 113, 115, 117, 121,
127, 129, 131, 133, 134, 162
chocolate, 2, 35–40, 43, 44, 46, 49, 52,
54–56 (see also food and meals)
chocolate heart, 2, 35, 36, 40, 43, 44, 46,
49, 52, 54, 56
Churchill, Winston, 69
Cicero, Marcus Tullius, 41
circle of friends, 69
circle of support, 69
clothing, 38, 44, 53, 65, 71, 103, 107, 109,
111
color, 12, 65, 100–103, 105–110, 113, 115,
117, 146, 149, 155
coloring books, 100, 102, 103, 161
comfort, 90, 95, 121, 127, 130, 131, 162,
163
comfort zone, 62, 63, 76
commitment, 47, 73, 82, 163
communication, 3, 6–8, 10, 41, 88, 94, 109
(see also nonverbal
communication)
enhancing, 9
written, 80–84, 137
communicator, 10
community, 134, 138
comparisons, 7, 143
compliments, 7
concern, 22, 52, 84
conclusions, 11, 134
confidence, 90
conflict, 13, 22, 32, 40, 88, 90, 92
connections, 1, 2, 29, 40–45, 49, 56, 82,
83, 126–128, 136, 138, 151, 153,
155, 157, 160
heart, 40
new, 106

social, 129
conscious, 12, 126, 130, 131 (see also mind)
consequences, 62
contact, 7, 9, 40–45, 55, 56, 114
contact sports, 41
contentment, 46
control, 18, 23, 24, 37, 74, 80, 82, 92, 93,
106, 112, 151, 164
coping skills, 68
couples, 7, 12, 48, 82, 106, 131, 163 (see
also husbands, marriage, and
wife)
courage, 8, 63, 93, 113, 163, 164
courtesies, 33
crayons, 2, 99–102, 105–108, 110–115,
117
craziness, 14, 42, 62, 82, 92
creativity, 2, 3, 11, 68, 70, 71, 84, 85, 101,
110–115, 149, 160, 162, 163,
165
crises, 67, 68, 143 (see also disasters)
criticism, 7, 12, 85, 110, 112
cuddling, 40, 45
curiosity, 90

**D**

damage, 66
dancing, 25, 50, 100, 103, 128, 163
DaVinci, Leonardo, 143
Davis, Bette, 135
*De Amicitia*, 41
de Chardin, Teilhard, 29
de Mello, Anthony, 63
De Rosis, Helen, 49
de Saint Exupery, Antoine, 52, 128
death, 24, 30, 31, 40, 60, 62, 127, 128,
145 (see also loss)
DeBono, Edward, 111
decisions, 12, 13, 23, 29, 62, 64
decorators, 107, 117
dedication, 47
deep breaths, 39, 73, 75, 81, 95 (see also
breathing)

Delta Society, 41

depression, 29, 37, 42, 72–74, 90, 108, 152

despondency, 42

destruction, 17, 23, 129

determination, 20, 90, 149

Dewar, Thomas, 11

Diana, Princess of Wales, 43

diary, 81 (see also journals)

direction, 64

disagreements, 11, 13, 90, 94

disarray, 106

disasters, 17, 106 (see also crises)

discouragement, 90

discoveries, 13, 30, 44, 49, 50, 52, 68, 81, 113, 129, 162

Disney, Walt, 61

distorted images, 42

distress, 7, 43

diversity, 146

doctors, 36, 72, 73, 87, 143

Doctorow, E.L., 80

dogs, 75 (see also animals, pets)

drawing, 2, 101, 112, 114

*Drawing on the Right Side of the Brain*, 114, 162

dreams, 24, 48, 61, 62, 69, 81, 82, 84, 138

Duke University, 29

Durfee, Cliff, 6

**E**

ears, 6, 7, 9, 33

earth, 72, 105, 108, 128, 151–155, 157

Earth Day, 154

Edison, Thomas, 16, 144

Edwards, Betty, 114

Einstein, Albert, 17, 28, 110

elastic band, 2, 59–61, 63, 66, 69, 72–74, 76

elderly, the, 44, 138 (see also senior)

embarrassment, 1, 90

embrace, 9, 61, 107 (see also hugs)

Emerson, 53

Emmanuel, 126

emotional baggage, 92

emotional distress, 43

emotional energy, 46

emotional release, 86, 89

emotional risk, 61

emotional support, 72

emotional touch, 43

emotions, 2, 17, 22, 31, 43–46, 61, 62, 65, 72, 80, 82, 84, 86–90, 93, 108, 113, 135

empathy, 44

endorphins, 121–123

endurance, 47

energy, 26, 30, 46, 49, 73, 74, 80, 87, 88, 108

enthusiasm, 1, 48, 90

envy, 90

eraser, 91–93

essential oils, 153, 156

euphoria, 46

evaluations, 24, 33

*Everyday Symbols for Joyful Living* workbook, 33

excitement, 85, 90, 105, 107

exercise, 45, 47, 72–76, 87, 112 (see also stretching and yoga)

existence, 28, 29

expenses, 14, 26 (see also finances, money, relationships with money, and spending)

experts, 9, 11, 69

extravagance, 26

extroverts, 62

exuberance, 46

eye contact, 7, 9

**F**

F.E.A.R., 63

facial expressions, 9 (see also body language and nonverbal communication)

failure, 68

faith, 3, 28, 31, 68 (see also beliefs, God, higher power, prayer and religion)
family, 1, 13, 14, 18–20, 32, 41, 42, 47, 48, 62, 81, 85, 100–102, 107, 111, 115, 120, 128, 129, 131, 134, 143, 161
family law attorney, 23
fantasies, 47, 101–103
fathers, 18, 23, 47, 120 (see also parents)
fear, 24, 40, 63, 68, 69, 82, 87, 90, 110, 163
FEAR trap, 63
feedback, 19, 42
feuds, 13
finances, 19, 23, 24, 26, 61, 62, 65, 81, 85, 87 (see also expenses, money, relationships with money, and spending)
financial planners, 23
"fine dining" sex, 48 (see also bedroom, the, libido, "make love," physical love, quickies, and sex)
flair, 149
flamboyance, 107
flavors, 39, 56
focus, 17, 46, 66, 81, 83, 85, 90, 106, 112, 122, 126, 130, 131, 133, 135, 137
foil wrapping, 40, 55
food, 26, 38, 48, 82, 95, 104, 129, 131 (see also chocolate and meals)
Ford, Linda, 49
forgiveness, 89, 91–96, 165
forgiveness list, 94
Franklin, Benjamin, 91
free association, 89
freedom, 12, 24, 165 (see also independence)
friends, 11, 13, 20, 23, 30, 32, 41, 44, 45, 48, 50, 53, 55, 64, 68, 69, 73, 87, 89, 93, 101, 102, 104, 107, 108, 114, 115, 124, 128, 129, 131, 134
Frost, Robert, 147
frustration, 42, 66

fun, 2, 49, 74, 100, 101, 109, 110, 122–124, 134, 162

## G

"game night," 102, 104
games, 102, 104, 122, 165
Gesundheit Institute, The, 122
gifts, 81, 93, 95, 113, 120, 124, 136, 147, 149, 152–154, 162, 163, 165, 166
Ginkgo, 152
Giovannoni, L., 23
goals, 24, 66, 68, 74
God, 17, 28, 30, 31, 126, 127, 136 (see also beliefs, faith, higher power, prayer, and religion)
gods, 31
Goldberg, Natalie, 81, 82
Gonzalez-Crussi, F., 127
good fortune, 16 (see also luck)
Goodman, Beth, 49
gratitude, 17, 24, 139
growth, 17, 18, 23, 30, 42, 49, 60, 62, 67, 68, 70, 84, 86, 112, 126, 129, 134, 135, 139, 142, 152, 160, 161
guidance counselors, 62

## H

Habitat for Humanity, 47
habits, 67, 95, 127, 130
Hagen, Walter, 101
handwritten letter, 87
happiness, 2, 17, 38, 46, 73, 87, 100, 102, 142, 164 (see also joy)
Harlow, Harry, 42
Harlow, Jean, 42
healing, 29, 30, 37, 42, 43, 87, 93, 108, 122, 152, 153, 160, 163–165
health, 12, 17, 18, 29, 32, 36–38, 40, 42, 43, 46, 48, 49, 65, 72, 74, 82, 86–88, 93, 106, 121, 131, 133, 134, 143, 145, 146, 153, 166 (see also well-being)

healthy model, 67
healthy relationships, 82, 106 (see also
    relationships)
hearing, 1, 6, 7, 12, 15, 18, 19
heart, 2, 6, 28, 29, 33, 35–38, 40, 41, 43,
    44, 46, 49, 52–54, 56, 63, 69, 82,
    92, 102, 121, 127, 164
"heart connection," 40
Hegel, G.W.F., 47
helplessness, 67, 90
Hershey's Kisses™, 46
higher power, 28, 30, 68 (see also beliefs,
    faith, God, prayer, and religion)
home, 14, 24, 41, 42, 83, 84, 102, 106,
    109, 111, 115, 116, 120, 138,
    142, 147, 149, 152, 160
honor, 6, 18, 130, 131, 133, 134
"honored person," 18
hope, 2, 29, 82, 84, 90, 94, 144, 164
Horace, 100
hostility, 22, 90
huggees, 42
huggers, 42
Hughes, Langston, 48
hugs, 41–45, 103, 163 (see also embrace)
"human moments," 43
humiliation, 90
humor, 3, 53, 68, 70, 71, 120–125, 166
    (see also jokes and laughter)
"humor carts," 122
hunches, 16, 113, 135 (see also inner voice
    and intuition)
hurt, 18, 88, 89, 92, 93, 95, 122, 139 (see
    also pain)
husbands, 24, 48, 68, 81, 134 (see also
    couples, marriage, and wife)
hypnosis, 112

## I

"I can" attitude, 20, 21, 33
*I Love Lucy,* 121, 124
"I love you," 9
immunity, 43

impulsiveness, 46, 61
"In God We Trust," 28, 30
"in love," 37 (see also love and romantic love)
incorporation, 3, 134, 136, 149
independence, 68, 70 (see also freedom)
influence, 24, 41, 70
initiative, 68, 70
inner child, 100, 113
inner voice, 12 (see also hunches and
    intuition)
inside, 23, 52–56, 103, 104, 110, 144, 152
insight, 2, 3, 30, 31, 33, 68, 70, 71, 81
inspiration, 1, 2, 102, 131, 135
intellect, 61, 62, 65
intellectual risk, 61, 65
intimacy, 22, 40, 42, 45, 48, 49, 82, 163
introvert, 62
intuition, 12, 15, 16, 108, 113 (see also
    hunches and inner voice)
isolation, 41, 42 (see also abandonment,
    alone, and loneliness)
issue, 10, 11, 13, 14, 22, 82, 87, 88, 143

## J

job, 6, 7, 14, 23, 54, 61, 64, 70, 81, 143
    (see also making a living, office,
    and work)
jokes, 72, 101, 120, 124, 163 (see also
    humor and laughter)
journals, 56, 76, 81, 82, 84, 86, 90, 94, 96,
    102, 117, 139, 157 (see also diary)
  family, 85
  personal, 84
  shared, 85
joy, 73, 102, 134, 153 (see also happiness)
judgment, 12, 90, 143

## K

Keller, Helen, 61
kindness, 18, 20
Kipling, Rudyard, 102
kisses, 41, 42, 45, 127

# L

labels, 17, 20, 114
"Laugh List," 124
*Laughing Matters* magazine, 121
laughter, 45, 86, 102, 120–124, 134, 139,
 148 (see also humor and jokes)
*Laws of Spirit, The,* 54
learning, 9, 10, 24, 26, 32, 41, 45, 50, 61,
 63, 66, 68, 69, 80–82, 85–87, 92,
 95, 101, 107, 108, 110–112, 114,
 125, 133, 135, 137, 151, 160–162
L'Engle, Madeleine, 133
letters, 7, 45, 64, 82, 87–90, 94
Levinson, Sam, 53
libido, 36 (see also bedroom, the, "fine
 dining" sex, "make love,"
 physical love, quickies, and sex)
life after death, 30, 31
life journey, 143
life script, 137
light, 49, 53, 74, 80, 92, 102, 106, 115,
 120–125, 152, 160
listener, 6, 10
literature, 29 (see also books)
*Little Prince, The,* 128
loneliness, 41, 44, 90 (see also
 abandonment, alone, and
 isolation)
"loneliness gap," 44
loss, 62, 66, 164 (see also death)
lost, 42, 49, 50, 53, 63, 67
love, 7, 9, 11, 18, 30, 36, 37, 39, 40, 44–
 48, 50, 52, 53, 61, 64, 65, 82, 83,
 90–93, 95, 102, 121, 124, 128,
 129, 131, 137, 147, 164 (see also
 "in love," and romantic love)
*Love Story,* 91, 137
luck, 16, 17, 19, 21, 165 (see also good
 fortune)
*Luck Factor, The,* 16, 165
lungs, 75

# M

*Magic Mandala Coloring Book,* 102
"make love," 45 (see also bedroom, the,
 "fine dining" sex, libido,
 physical love, quickies, and sex)
makeover, 53
making a living, 23, 47 (see also job, office
 and work)
mandalas, 102
marriage, 1, 12, 22, 23, 48, 62, 82, 120,
 128, 132, 145, 162 (see also
 couples, husbands, and wife)
marriage counseling, 12, 22, 48
massage, 43, 45, 49, 111
meals, 30, 102 (see also food)
 breakfast, 128
 dinner, 10, 101, 102, 128, 130
 lunch, 45, 114, 128
meanness, 18
meaning, 1, 2, 29, 83, 130, 132, 162
meaningful existence, 29
medication, 72, 86, 121, 153
meditation, 28, 29, 31, 61, 65, 102, 163
meetings, 72, 114
memoirs, 83
memories, 2, 17, 38, 87, 134, 138
menopause, 73, 74
mental focus, 46
mental health, 72
mentors, 44, 69, 138 (see also role models)
Millay, Edna St. Vincent, 63
Miller, Henry, 46
Millman, Dan, 54, 164
Mills, Joyce, 112, 114
mind, the, 2, 6, 7, 11, 12, 14, 16, 22, 72,
 81, 82, 95, 110, 144, 152, 153,
 157
mindset, 16
mirror, 13, 37, 94, 135, 149, 152
miscommunication, 82
mistake, 17, 91, 94, 95, 143
money, 14, 22–26, 33, 61, 106, 155, 165
 (see also expenses, finances,

relationships with money, and
spending)
money dynamics, 22, 23, 25–27
money management course, 24
mood, 72, 81, 109
morality, 68, 70
mother, 1, 18, 23, 29, 30, 42, 47, 81, 82,
92, 102, 127, 129, 151–155, 161
(see also parents)
Mother Nature, 151–155
Mother Teresa, 18, 30, 92
motivation, 1
movies, 26, 50, 91, 103, 137
muscles, 42, 74
music, 29, 47, 49, 50, 65, 74, 116

# N

naps, 144, 145 (see also "catnaps," rest,
and sleep)
Native Americans, 12, 135, 151
nature, 29, 30, 40, 41, 44, 66, 82, 105, 122,
126, 131, 135, 136, 151–155
nature walk, 44, 155
Navajo, Edward A., 106
negativity, 7, 18, 20, 86, 88, 113
negative comment, 18
negative label, 20
neighbors, 12, 43, 75, 138
neighborhood, 116
"Never Fake It Again" parties, 101
"Never Fake Your Artistic Ability,"
101
"Never Fake Your Football
Knowledge," 101
"Never Fake Your Serenity," 101
Newman, Candace, 153, 156 (see also oil
lady, the)
Nin, Anais, 60
nonverbal communication, 40 (see also
body language, communication,
and facial expressions)
"Nun Study, The," 134

# O

obstacles, 66
offense, 10, 94
office, 24, 63, 83, 87, 102, 116, 120, 142,
144, 149, 153 (see also job,
making a living, and work)
oil lady, the, 153 (see also Newman,
Candace)
olfactory science, 152 (see also scents and
smell)
Omega Institute, 55
opportunities, 44, 55, 64, 67, 68, 112, 154
optimism, 17, 19, 90 (see also positive)
options, 14, 29, 63
order, 28, 89, 100, 106, 109, 111, 127
our bodies, 37, 121, 135
out of control, 82, 106
overwhelmed, 2
"other infidelity, the," 23 (see also money)
*Owner's Manual, The*, 49
Oz, Dr. Mehmet C., 143

# P

pain, 24, 43, 60, 66, 87–89, 92, 121, 122,
142, 152 (see also hurt)
parallels, 64, 106
paranoia, 90
parents, 23, 26, 42, 69, 87, 131 (see also
fathers and mother)
partners, 7, 45, 50, 75, 87, 128
passion, 40, 46–51, 56, 100, 108, 163
"passion deprivation," 48
passion priority list, 48
passion reality list, 48
past, 23, 28, 70, 126, 135, 165
pastime, 110
Pauling, Linus, 12
paying attention, 7, 12, 21, 22, 25
peace, 17, 47, 90, 112, 135, 164, 165
peaceful environment, 17
pencil, 2, 79–81, 83–89, 91, 93, 95, 96,
102, 134

penny, 2, 5–9, 11, 13, 15–17, 19, 21–31, 33
permission, 41, 93, 102, 107
persecution, 28
perseverance, 62
personal ad, 55
personal environment, 106
perspectives, 3, 12, 13, 113 (see also viewpoint)
pets, 41, 45 (see also animals and dogs)
photos, 155 (see also pictures)
physical, 27, 31, 40–43, 45, 55, 61, 62, 65, 72, 74, 87, 121, 134
  boundaries, 41
  caring, 40
  health, 74, 134
  love, 40
  risk, 61, 65
Picasso, Pablo, 112
pictures, 1, 55, 100, 103, 108, 109, 112, 114, 138, 150 (see also photos)
planning, 23, 48, 49, 50, 51, 62, 64, 67, 75, 102, 109
play, 28, 31, 36, 41, 47, 50, 65, 100–105, 112, 113, 129, 133
pleasures, 38, 39, 153
point of view, 12
polyphenol flavonoids, 37
Ponder, Catherine, 22
positive, 3, 7, 16–20, 33, 42, 67, 70, 83, 85, 86, 121, 131, 133, 134, 137, 143, 164, 166 (see also optimism)
  comments, 18, 19
  feedback, 19
  memories, 134
  physical feedback, 42
  thinking, 3, 17, 143
*Positive Thinking Magazine*, 143
power, 1, 2, 16, 24, 28, 30, 36, 68, 80, 87, 112, 135, 151–153, 164
Powys, Llewelyn, 107
praise, 18, 19
prayer, 29–31, 131 (see also beliefs, faith, God, higher power and religion)

predictions, 15
pretending, 26, 67, 89, 115
pride, 68, 90, 147
principles, 3, 165
private, 22, 28, 62, 101, 144
problems, 7, 11, 14, 37, 48, 66, 81, 87, 106, 112–115, 129, 144, 153
problem-solving, 112, 113, 115, 144
protection, 142, 143, 145 (see also safety and security)
Proust, Marcel, 30
Proverbs 24:16, 68
psychiatrist, 68
psychologists, 68
psychology, 41, 66, 164

**Q**

quickies, 48 (see also bedroom, the, "fine dining" sex, libido, "make love," physical love, and sex)

**R**

rage, 86, 88, 89, 94 (see also anger and unresolved anger)
"reaction mode," 88
reality, 16, 37, 48, 80, 121, 135
rebound, 68
reconnection, 45, 49
recreation, 122
"Red Plate Ritual," 130
reflection, 135, 136
regret, 90
relationships, 8, 11, 18, 22–25, 33, 48, 52, 69, 82, 88, 92, 106, 128, 135, 143, 151, 154, 163 (see also healthy relationships)
  with money, 22, 24, 25, 33 (see also expenses, finances, money, and spending)
relaxation, 20, 29, 42, 43, 48, 49, 75, 95, 100, 143, 144, 165
relaxation response, 29

relief, 90, 152, 153
religion, 28, 31, 32, 102 (see also beliefs, faith, God, higher power, and prayer)
renaming, 20
research, 1, 17, 18, 29, 37, 42, 43, 64, 66, 68, 69, 86, 121, 143, 152
    AMA Research Study, 43
    brain, 1
resiliency, 16, 66–71, 121, 165 (see also bouncing back and snapping back)
    inventory, 70
*Resilient Self, The*, 68, 165
resistance, 60
resolutions, 11
respect, 12, 18, 151
responsibility, 7, 48
rest, 43, 63, 144, 145, 157 (see also "catnaps," naps, and sleep)
retirement, 44, 47, 130, 138
retreats, 54, 55, 61
revenge, 92
Rilke, Rainer Maria, 53
risk, 60–65, 134
    chart, 64
    financial, 61
rite of passage, 129
rituals, 36, 72, 126–132, 161–163 (see also traditions)
    bedtime, 131
    celebration, 126
    holiday, 132
Roizen, Dr. Michael F., 143
role models, 43, 47, 111, 135, 137, 138 (see also mentors)
romantic love, 46, 91 (see also "in love" and love)
Roosevelt, Eleanor, 63
rough times, 68, 70

**S**

sad, 23, 41, 73, 84, 86, 87, 89, 90

safety, 41, 69, 82, 127, 143 (see also protection and security)
Satir, Virgini, 42
satisfaction, 42, 85, 90
scents, 39, 49, 152 (see also olfactory science and smell)
scripting, 84, 137
scripting technique, 137
scriptures, 29
Seattle, Chief, 152
seasonal affective disorder (SAD), 152
seashells, 2, 141–149, 151, 153–155, 157
secrets, 6, 22–24, 166
security, 24, 127, 128 (see also protection and safety)
self-criticism, 85
self-esteem, 41, 61, 146
self-inventory, 54
self-validation, 85
selfishness, 92
senior, 137 (see also elderly, the)
serenity, 74, 101, 102
"serenity bags," 101
serotonin, 37
sex, 22, 23, 36, 40, 42, 48, 49, 87 (see also bedroom, the, "fine dining" sex, libido, "make love," physical love, and quickies)
shyness, 90
silence, 18, 30, 135, 136, 155
simplicity, 3, 7, 10, 15, 43, 81, 83, 92, 105, 106, 113, 130, 153, 160–162
situations, 13, 64, 70, 87, 121, 132
skin, 41, 42, 142, 143, 162
sleep, 115, 143–145 (see also "catnaps," naps and rest)
sleep-deprivation, 143
smell, 39, 92, 101, 105, 106, 153, 155, 156 (see also scents and olfactory science)
snapping back, 76 (see also bouncing back and resiliency)
social services, 122
society, 2, 17, 30, 40–42, 44, 53, 73, 86,

87, 107, 128, 129, 131, 133, 143, 146

solitude, 54, 135, 136

solutions, 7, 112–115, 144

sorry, 18, 90–94, 96 (see also apologies)

soul, 28–30, 37, 43, 44, 54, 121, 162, 163

speaker, 1, 6

speaking, 7, 9, 17, 20, 28, 29, 66, 82, 85, 93, 111, 115

spending, 20, 24, 26, 31, 52, 106, 111, 114, 115, 138, 146, 154 (see also expenses, finances, money, and relationships with money)

spiritual insight, 31, 33

spiritual inventory, 31

spiritual knowledge, 30

spiritual mission statement, 31

spiritual risk, 61

spirituality, 28–33, 55, 61, 62, 65, 108, 134, 162, 164–166

*Spirituality & Health* magazine, 32

spouse, 20, 41, 55, 87, 109, 128

strategists, 68

strength, 12, 68, 83, 93, 147

stress, 29, 83, 133, 134, 144, 152 (see also anxiety)

stretching, 2, 60–64, 72–75, 77, 144 (see also exercise and yoga)

stubbornness, 20, 90

students, 1, 2, 11

styles, 65, 129, 149

substance abuse, 43

suffering, 18, 48, 66, 88, 143, 153

Sufi, 53, 87

Sufi Teaching, 87

suicide, 43

support, 62, 68, 69, 72

support groups, 72

support systems, 62

survivors, 68, 69, 165

"Survivor's Pride," 68

suspicion, 90

"Switch Hands Technique," 114

"symbols of serenity" bag, 102

### T

talent, 149

talk, 6, 7, 9, 11, 30, 47–49, 61, 62, 65, 82, 84, 88, 95, 102, 106, 121, 127–129, 137

teachers, 17, 23, 62, 110

teenagers, 2, 42, 129 S(see also adolescence)

television, 53, 121 (see also TV)

Templeton, Sir John, 30

tension, 42, 61, 74

thank-you note, 149

therapists, 1, 22, 41, 42, 53, 73, 111, 112, 153

therapy, 7, 18, 65, 69, 81, 87, 106, 120, 152, 153, 161, 163, 165

thoughts, 6–9, 12, 28, 31, 33, 38, 80, 90, 93, 96, 110

Tillich, Paul, 7

time out, 13

*Today Show, The*, 47

tone, 9, 10, 65, 82

touch, 2, 30, 40–43, 45, 72, 75, 153, 155

"touch void," 41

toxicity, 88, 90, 164

traditions, 122, 127–129, 164 (see also rituals)

traditional medicine, 122

transcendence, 66

transformation, 1, 29, 48, 52, 120, 130, 164, 165

transition, 128–130, 143 (see also change)

trauma, 69, 87

tricks, 88, 100, 101

trust, 8, 28–31

Tunney, Gene, 73

TV, 9 (see also television)

### U

uncensored, 89

unconscious, 12, 84, 126, 131

undecided, 90

uniqueness, 1, 146–150, 157
universities, 29
unkind words, 18
unresolved anger, 88 (see also anger and rage)

**V**

Valentine's Day, 46
value, 7, 17, 23, 24, 26, 28, 30, 43, 53, 82, 130, 133, 136, 139, 160
victim model, 66
videos, 75, 122, 124
viewpoint, 11–13 (see also perspectives)
violence, 42, 43
vision, 11, 12, 54, 85
visualization, 12, 89, 95
visualization technique, 95
volunteering, 44, 45
vulnerability, 93, 143, 145

**W**

web of life, 152
well-being, 41, 152 (see also health)
wellness programs, 122
wife, 48, 101 (see also couples, husbands, and marriage)
win-lose, 13
win-win, 13
wind, 66, 92, 154, 155
wisdom, 3, 54, 81, 133, 135, 136
Wiseman, Richard, 16
wit, 120
withdrawal, 90, 142
Wolin, Steve, M.D., 68, 165
Wolin, Sybil, Ph.D., 68, 165
women, 23, 36, 52, 53, 62, 107, 130, 134, 163–165
work, 1, 2, 9, 12–14, 16, 18, 24, 47, 48, 62, 63, 65, 68, 69, 73, 74, 80, 85, 91–93, 100, 105, 106, 111, 115, 120, 128, 134, 143, 144, 153, 163 (see also job, making a living, and office)

workbook, 33, 164
World War II, 23
writing, 14, 23, 26, 28, 31, 33, 37, 45, 47, 55, 64, 70, 73, 80–92, 94, 109, 114, 115, 130, 134, 137, 149
"writing timeout," 88, 90
written communication, 80–85, 137
written reality, 80
written word, 82, 83
websites, 55, 155, 156, 166
    www.albinarts.com, 155, 166
    www.ciweb.org, 166
    www.eomega.org, 55, 166
    www.goodmedicinetin.com, 156, 166
    www.humorproject.com, 125, 166
    www.kerismith.com, 166
    www.makethedashcount.com, 166
    www.marthabartfeld.com, 166
    www.positivethinkingmag.com, 166
    www.templetonpress.com, 166
    www.thetwelvegifts.com, 166

**Y**

yawning, 73, 75
yoga, 75 (see also exercise and stretching)

# About the Author

Photo courtesy of Memories and Milestones

Three generations of joyful living: *The author (left), her mother, Ami, and daughter, Kirsten, celebrate Ami's 95th birthday.*

**Dianne Durante, Ed.S.,** is an expert on marriage, family, and the educational system. She has more than 35 years of experience as a therapist and educator, has hosted her own radio talk show, and is the author of numerous grants and articles.

One of her first grants is now a unique self-guided self-esteem program called *Circle of Hearts,* used by churches and community groups to build stronger communities through connection. Her motivational columns have been published worldwide in business, lifestyle and educational publications.

A member of the prestigious National Speakers Association, Dianne is known nationwide for her innovative, interactive presentations, which combine symbols and stories to keep audiences laughing as they learn to remember the basics for living a happy life.

Dianne has created and conducted parent education programs for the traditional and blended family, as well as support groups for divorced parents and children of divorce. She has taught psychology and sociology courses at the university level on topics such as women, aging, wellness, death, and love. She was a member of one of the first Critical Incident Stress Debriefing teams sent to Oklahoma City to help survivors of the Oklahoma City bombing. Dianne also volunteers for the American Red Cross, counseling those affected by hurricanes and other natural disasters.

Dianne completed her degree as an Educational Specialist in Marriage and Family Therapy at Seton Hall University in South Orange, New Jersey. She earned her Masters of Education in Counseling Education at William Paterson College in Wayne, New Jersey, and her Bachelor of Science in Education/Psychology from the University of Dayton in Ohio. She has received advanced training in Women, Family Systems, and Alcohol Studies from Rutgers University of Medicine and Dentistry, New Jersey, in addition to training in Ericksonian Hypnosis and NeuroLinguistic Programming. She is a clinical member of the American Association of Marriage and Family Therapists, the Florida Counseling Association, Nationally Certified Counselors, and the American Orthopsychiatric Association.

Born and raised in Chicago, Dianne moved to the New York/New Jersey area to further her education in 1969. She currently resides in Naples, Fla., where she runs a rewarding and successful counseling practice. She loves the beach, the color purple, her work, and her family.

Look for her upcoming books, *Everyday Symbols for Surviving Grief* and *Everyday Symbols for Passionate Parenting.*

---

*The author would love to hear about your personal meaning for these symbols as well as any other symbols that enrich your life. Please send your ideas and insights to:*

Dianne Durante, Ed.S., Director
Anchor Counseling and Training Center
812 Anchor Rode Drive
Naples, FL 34103

*Or contact the author through her publisher:*

Email to: Durante@QoLpublishing.com
Call toll-free in U.S. & Canada: 1-877-513-0099
Local: 239-513-9907

# About the Illustrator

The illustrator and one of her beagles, Frances, mug for the camera.

**Kelly Cabrera**, born in South Korea and raised in Waterloo, N.Y., discovered at a very early age that she had a knack for drawing and an eye for detail.

Her very first preschool art project was a self portrait that depicted her exactly as she was outfitted for the day, from the multi-colored striped turtle neck, right down to her mis-matched shoelaces. Little Kelly was the very last to finish, painstakingly recreating herself with butcher paper and jumbo crayons, until she reluctantly stopped when the teacher could wait no longer.

She is the illustrator of *Circle of Hearts* by Dianne Durante and is working on several self-help books to be published by Quality of Life Publishing in 2008 and 2009.

Kelly now lives in Naples, Fla., with her fiancé, Kevin, and her four beloved pets, Benny, Frances, Sophie and Jack.

# How to Order

Quality of Life Publishing Co. specializes in inspirational and gentle grief support books for readers of all ages. Here's how to order *Everyday Symbols for Joyful Living* and other publications:

**Bookstores:**     Available wherever books are sold.

**Email:**     **books@QoLpublishing.com**

**Phone:**     **1-877-513-0099**
Toll-free in the U.S. and Canada
or call 1-239-513-9907.
Call during regular business hours Eastern Time.

**Fax:**     **1-239-513-0088**

**Mail:**     **Quality of Life Publishing Co.**
P.O. Box 112050
Naples, FL 34108-1929

Look for Dianne Durante's upcoming books, *Everyday Symbols for Surviving Grief* and *Everyday Symbols for Passionate Parenting.*